The
INCLUSIVE
SCHOOL

Sustaining
Equity and Standards

The
INCLUSIVE
SCHOOL

Sustaining Equity and Standards

Judy W. Kugelmass

Teachers College, Columbia University
New York and London

Published by Teachers College Press, 1234 Amsterdam Avenue, New York, NY 10027

Copyright © 2004 by Teachers College, Columbia University

Library of Congress Cataloging-in-Publication Data
Kugelmass, Judy W.
  The inclusive school: sustaining equity and standards / Judy W. Kugelmass.
    p. cm.
  Includes bibliographical references and index.
  ISBN 0-8077-4492-1 (cloth) — ISBN 0-8077-4491-3 (pbk.)
    1. Inclusive education—United States—Case studies.   2. Children with disabilities—Education (Elementary)—United States—Case studies.   3. Children of minorities—Education (Elementary)—United States—Case studies.
  I. Title.
  LC1201.K84   2004
  371.9'046—dc22   2004053725

ISBN 0-8077-4491-3 (paper)
ISBN 0-8077-4492-1 (cloth)

Printed on acid-free paper

Manufactured in the United States of America

11 10 09 08 07 06   8 7 6 5 4 3 2

To Anna Rhea and
Ezra Josh Kugelmass Austin

Contents

Acknowledgments

This book would not have been possible without the teachers and principals who invited me into their classrooms and schools. These warriors of compassion are unrelenting in their struggle to create educational settings that are responsive to every child. Each of their stories illustrates the delicate balancing act they perform by remaining committed to public education, in spite of policies that are not in the best interest of children. I regret not being able to acknowledge individuals by name but must instead respect their requests for confidentiality. Thus all names of teachers, principals, and schools are pseudonyms.

I want to acknowledge the many international colleagues who provided opportunities to examine inclusive school cultures beyond the limited borders of an American imagination, enabling me to place what I found at Betsy Miller into a broader context. These people include colleagues in Eastern Europe—Alvyra Galkiene and Danius Puras in Lithuania and Natalia Sofi in Ukraine—and Ana Maria Benard da Costa and her staff at the Institute for Educational innovation in Portugal. Also, Mel Ainscow and the faculty and staff in the Department of Inclusion and Educational Support at the University of Manchester provided important feedback on my research and opened doors to British schools and beyond. I am most grateful to Averil Gould for the secretarial and emotional support she provided during my stay in Manchester. I also want to acknowledge the National College for School Leadership for supporting my stay in the United Kingdom and facilitating the comparative study of leadership in inclusive schools discussed in the concluding chapter of this book.

Several people provided research and editorial assistance during the years it took to complete this book. The hours Lizabeth Cain spent transcribing interview tapes did more than provide research assistance. It inspired her to become the kind of teacher-warrior who now inspires children. Bill Lee gathered and organized archival data related to the closing of Harold Dodge and its merger with Betsy Miller, adding the perspectives of individuals I was unable to meet in person. I also want to thank Roberta Wallit for reading and commenting on an earlier draft of the book's manuscript and providing editorial assistance. Elizabeth Bloom's reading of the final manuscript provided additional editorial assistance and feedback from a teacher who, like those at Betsy Miller, understands that teaching is about saving children's lives.

I have been examining the cultures of schools and discussing the ideas presented in the following pages with friends, family, colleagues, and students for many years. These individuals helped shape this book. I am particularly grateful to colleagues at Binghamton University who read early versions of the book's manuscript. Professors Barbara Regenspan and Sue Crowley offered important insights into feminism and progressive pedagogy and helped clarify my writing. Professor Beverley Rainforth kept me focused on the needs of children with severe disabilities when considering inclusive school cultures. I also want to thank my dear friends Rich and Diane Farnham for introducing me to spiritual teachings that expanded my understanding of the primacy of compassion in creating inclusive schools. Last but not least, I want to thank my lifelong partner, Hal Kugelmass, for his endless hours of reading, editing, and critiquing the many incarnations of this book, and especially for his unconditional love.

*You must be the change
you wish to see in the world.*
—Mohandas K. Gandhi

CHAPTER 1

Educational Reform and the Creation of a Culture of Inclusion

Progressive social reformers have struggled with political conservatives, fundamentalist religious groups, and business interests for ownership of public education since its inception. Each side has presented its reform agenda in terms of what is best for children when, in fact, all have been driven by adult concerns originating far beyond the walls of the schoolhouse. The story of the elementary school described in this book, the Betsy Miller Elementary School, demonstrates how one group of teachers responded to the continual shifts reflected in changing ideologies among educational policy makers during the closing years of the twentieth century. This is not a fairy tale with a happily-ever-after ending. There will be no hero or heroine to save the day. Rather, it is a story of teachers, administrators, and parents struggling to sustain a public school in which *success* is defined more broadly than the attainment of predetermined academic standards on high-stakes tests.

Success involves much more than academic achievement. It also means getting along with others, solving problems, thinking critically, contributing to the school and community, and attaining personal fulfillment and happiness. This broadened definition does not require scientific measurement or experimentally designed research to demonstrate to teachers and parents that students are learning and growing intellectually, physically, emotionally, socially, and spiritually. Teachers need not rely on comparing one child to another or use student's ability to meet externally imposed criteria to assess progress in their classrooms. Reliable information about children emerges through authentic relationships teachers establish with students and families. Children's capacities and achievements then become obvious through lived experiences and interactions with one another, everyday. Growth and development can be monitored and documented by systematic observations of children's work, behavior, and interactions with peers and adults (Carini, 2001; Himley & Carini, 2000).

Children attending Betsy Miller are required to take statewide standardized tests. In 2001 and 2002, 82% of its fourth graders were at or above the expected learning standards for language arts as compared to 66% statewide of students at comparable schools; 84% were at or above the expected standards for math as compared to 76% statewide. These scores have been used both to indicate that the school is doing a good job when compared to others serving a similarly diverse student body and to draw attention to the 14–18% of its students who are failing to reach the learning standards set by the state. Teachers at Betsy Miller look beyond these test scores to assess the progress of their students. Although concerned when students do poorly on standardized tests, their focus is directed at addressing the daily struggles and challenges many children face at home, in the community, and in school.

The story that follows demonstrates how the vagaries of public policy impact teachers' ability to sustain authentic assessment processes, as well as the inclusive culture they reflect. The teachers whose voices are presented in this book discover that although they are empowered individuals operating out of a strong sense of commitment to children and public education, they can neither effect change nor sustain their school's culture as lone rangers. Their story will reveal the importance of engaging in collaborative decision making and collective action. At Betsy Miller, these collaborations supported both the assessment and instructional practices teachers developed for a very diverse group of students, and the schoolwide policies needed to sustain these practices. Collective action would help combat threats to the sustainability of their work emanating from outside the school, compel each teacher to reflect on her or his assumptions about what is best for kids, and at times require uncomfortable compromises. Their stories will resonate with others confronting similar situations and hopefully inspire reflection and collective action directed toward the creation and sustainability of inclusive schools.

Although this school's evolution may resemble that of others, the specific strategies used by the staff at Betsy Miller for addressing the challenges they faced can never be precisely duplicated. That is not the purpose of this book. Rather, its intent is to provide a broad and flexible template of collaborative processes, practices and structures, commitments and beliefs that need to be molded to fit other contexts. The story that unfolds in the coming chapters will hopefully motivate other educators in their struggle to create and sustain democratic and inclusive public schools. Regardless of their resources, location, and population, all schools can be places where children remain at the center of adult decisions. This requires teachers and administrators who are guided by an unconditional acceptance of every child. The descriptions of day-to-day life at Betsy Miller that follow will demonstrate how one group of teachers and their principal attempted to hold on to this ethos in the face of constant challenges.

A BROADENED DEFINITION OF INCLUSIVE SCHOOLS

The definition of *inclusion* used throughout this book is conceptualized more broadly than is typical in the United States. Rather than focusing only on the education of children with disabilities and others with special educational needs, inclusive education is understood as a philosophy supporting and celebrating diversity in its broadest sense. This understanding reflects a definition of inclusion supported by UNESCO and adopted in developing nations as well as those with established educational infrastructures and traditions. Inclusive schools are designed to secure children's basic human right to an individually, culturally, and developmentally appropriate education and to eliminate social exclusion (UNESCO, 1997, 2000). The central features of inclusion that follow from this broadened definition are listed in Figure 1.1

In the United Kingdom, inclusive schools are defined as educational institutions designed to promote active participation among all students in the culture and curricula of the school, and in their local communities. Creating this kind of school has required the intentional restructuring of school cultures, policies, and practices in both the United Kingdom and the United States (Booth & Ainscow, 1998; Keogh, 1988; Lipsky & Gartner, 1996). A comparative review of school programs in the United States where curricular innovations, school organization, and classroom structures were designed to accommodate diversity in learning and behavior among children with special educational needs demonstrates the effectiveness of this kind of school for the academic achievement and social development of all students (Manset & Semmel, 1997).

My commitment to the development of inclusive schools began in 1978 while I was at Syracuse University supervising student teachers and school psychologists at the Jowonio School. This university-affiliated, early-childhood and elementary school demonstrated that it was possible to integrate systematic approaches to instruction for children with autism, severe emotional disturbances, and other pervasive developmental disorders within a progressively oriented, intellectually, aesthetically, and emotionally rich environment that included typically developing children. Through my interactions with children, families, and teachers, I witnessed the positive impact such a setting could have on the lives of children and adults (Biklen, 1985;

FIGURE 1.1. A Broadened Definition of Inclusion (Adapted from UNESCO 1997; 2000)

1. All children attend the same schools and receive instruction in the same classes they would attend if not disabled or educationally disadvantaged.
2. Remedial, special education, and related services are provided within general education settings. Specialists work closely with classroom teachers to support all students and provide adaptations and specialized interventions to ensure successful participation and learning in the general education environment and curriculum.
3. When needed, accommodations are made in the general education curriculum so that all students attain skills appropriate to their chronological age and developmental needs.
4. The curriculum is conceived as promoting social-emotional and developmental growth, as well as providing instruction designed to help students meet age appropriate and grade-level learning standards in all academic areas.
5. All students are held to high expectations, while recognizing the need for individualization.
6. Classrooms are learning communities, in which all students are valued members who support one another.
7. Diversity in culture, language, ability, and student interests are all celebrated and are seen as enriching the educational experiences of all children.
8. Families are active and integral members of the school community.

Knoblock, 1982, 1996). These experiences provided a model for what was possible and enabled me to see the importance of progressive school reform to the creation of schools that served *all* children.

After leaving Jowonio in 1980, I did not, until 1994, find a public school where the majority of general education teachers were as deeply committed to including children with disabilities and other special educational needs in their classrooms. Although many conscientious and caring teachers were committed to supporting diversity among their students, most believed that children with disabilities were qualitatively different. Many pointed to obstacles created by the bureaucratic structures of both general and special education as limiting their ability to serve all children in their classrooms. These teachers knew what scholars investigating failed attempts at school reform had also been saying, namely, that the repeated failure of educational reforms reflected policy makers' lack of attention to the everyday life of teachers and children (Fullan, 1991; Fuller & Clark,

1994; Hargreaves, 1994; Sarason, 1996). Centralized bureaucracies continued to act as if teachers would obediently implement shifting and often contradictory demands when, in fact, they had historically resisted imposed reforms.

I was interested in finding teachers in public schools who did not resist reforms that promoted inclusion in its broadest sense. These teachers would need to sustain their commitments to both learner-centered practices and the inclusion of children with special educational needs in spite of bureaucratic challenges and obstacles. My continuing search for such a school eventually led to Betsy Miller. It was my hope that documenting and reporting what went on there might reveal strategies other teachers could adapt in order to promote both progressive reforms and inclusive education in other contexts.

THE BETSY MILLER ELEMENTARY SCHOOL

The participation of five teachers from Betsy Miller in one of my off-campus graduate courses introduced me to their work. These teachers along with the others in my introductory course on the Foxfire approach (Foxfire Fund, 1991) were asked to reflect on the relationship between engaging children in authentic choices and their own teaching (Dewey, 1938). The reflective journal of one European American woman from Betsy Miller, Karen Shriver, revealed a passionate and insightful struggle with issues concerning the empowerment of young children in her very diverse second-grade classroom. The following excerpt from her journal offers one of many examples of this struggle:

> I was very frustrated because I felt that the groups were floundering again. I am wondering if my worrying about being too directive has caused me to distance too far from the group. It looks as if I need to find a balance between guidance and takeover.
>
> I conferred with each group so I could get a better understanding of how I could best help. . . . Reviewing my observations and reading [the students'] written reflections made me recognize the need to have a discussion [with them] about what makes a good working group. I also decided it would be helpful to give each group a goal to work on for the week.
>
> Even though I'm not always successful helping students when the situation arises in class, I do go home and use their daily logs, reflective journals, and my observations to provide guidance for the next day.

Karen continues to reflect on the need to achieve a balance between teacher direction and student choice and, after 15 years of teaching, finds each new group of children requires her to behave differently than any other. When we first met, she had been at Betsy Miller for 7 years. When she invited me to visit her classroom and provide feedback on her teaching, I jumped at the chance to learn more about how she accommodated those students in her classroom who were nonnative speakers of English and others classified as eligible to receive special education services. These visits began in the fall of 1994 and continued until the spring of 1996. Our relationship would eventually lead to the 5 years of intensive fieldwork that provide the foundation for this book. I would continue to follow the impact of federal, state, and school district policy on the school until December 2002.

In the chapters that follow, I describe Karen's classroom and the ways it resembled others at the school from 1994–1996. The voices of other teachers then tell how they came to Betsy Miller, their participation in its development, and why, after 15 years (1987–2002), they remain uncertain of the school's ability to sustain its progressively oriented, inclusive culture. Their struggle is a consequence of more and more incompatible demands from a school system intending to assure educational equity while simultaneously requiring conformity to externally imposed standards. These demands for accountability through high-stakes testing have created a crisis Betsy Miller's teachers share with others trying to sustain schools that serve *all* children.

SCHOOL REFORM AND INCLUSION

Although corporations claim to have rejected much of what is associated with the factory model of production that guided the development of public schools at the beginning of the twentieth century, many of the same underlying values continue to guide corporate cultures and public education systems (Tyack & Cuban, 1995). Concerns for developing a product with predictable qualities has led both corporate culture and public school systems to establish uniform standards as criteria for assessing what is believed to be evidence of the quality of their mass-produced goods. Although new technologies allow for the possibility of more diversity in production and maintenance of quality control, this kind of customization is reserved for high-end consumers, not the general public. For those willing and able to pay, all kinds of accommodations are possible, while most others settle for one-size-fits-all methods of production.

Evidence of problems associated with assessments that look only at discrete qualities of a product rather than considering the specific contexts in which it operates can be found in both industrial practice and public education. The breakdown of Bridgestone-Firestone tires on Ford Explorers, under certain conditions of tire inflation, speed, and road surfaces is one example in the corporate world. By examining the qualities of each product in isolation from the other and not considering their interactions in specific contexts, both Ford and Firestone failed to provide valid or reliable assessments of the safety of their combined products.

In public education, the overrepresentation of minority children, particularly African American males, among those identified with mild disabilities (i.e., learning disabilities, behavioral and emotional disturbances) or in need of remediation offers another example of the unintended consequence of decontextualized and standardized assessment processes. In spite of evidence that reliance on standardized tests of achievement and intelligence leads to the inappropriate identification of disproportionate numbers of minority children as having a disability or being otherwise less able (Kirp, 1973/1992; Kugelmass, 1987; Larry P. v. Riles, 1972; Lytle, 1988/1992), this practice continues. In New York State, for example, not only are disproportionate numbers of minority students identified, as compared to White students with disabilities, but a larger percentage of minority students identified as having a disability are placed in more restrictive settings than their White counterparts (New York State, 1999). These kinds of classrooms offer few, if any, opportunities for interactions with higher achieving peers, limiting opportunities for positive social interactions and intellectual stimulation (Shea & Bauer, 1995). Placement in special education and remedial programs lowers expectations among teachers and parents and increases the chance that a student will drop out of school (Macmillan, Keogh, & Jones, 1986).

The requirement that all young children in public schools be assessed by standardized tests has, by 2003, become central to educational reforms in both the United States and England. The failure of national testing programs to bring about changes that assure educational equity for children living in poverty and/or from nondominant cultures has neither led the English government to rethink this flawed policy nor diminished its influence (Docking, 2000). Instead, the United States has followed British footsteps, imposing even more requirements for standardized testing under the Bush administration than those of preceding governments. Evidence that teachers resort to teaching to the test and ignore instructional practices that stimulate higher order thinking and reasoning when required to use test scores as a way to monitor performance (Worthen, 1993) has been ignored. Rather than raising the bar, standardized testing has historically led schools into patterns of maintaining minimal standards (Wiggins, 1989, 1991).

Eligibility for federal assistance to schools serving children from low-income families now requires local educational agencies' participation in the National Assessment for Educational Progress (NAEP) and their respective states' development of "a single, statewide accountability system" (No Child Left Behind Act, 2002). Although standardized tests are inadequate tools for obtaining valid and reliable information about children whose life circumstances provide contexts not envisioned by test makers (Shea & Bauer, 1995), poor performance on these assessments can be used to penalize schools serving children whose needs go far beyond their poor academic performance.

Children in publicly supported schools receive additional support only when they are unable to successfully negotiate the mandated curriculum. If their failure is determined to be the result of a specific set of factors defined as evidence of a disability, they become classified as eligible for special education. When academic problems are not classifiable, but the child attends a school with a significant low-income population in the United States, she or he can receive remedial services funded by Title 1 of the Elementary and Secondary Education Act, now called the No Child Left Behind Act (NCLB). Services provided under either Title 1 or special education programs are generally built on instructional models that were designed to remedy deficits. The success of some of these approaches for skill remediation and behavior control has led to the proliferation of a behavioral paradigm in special education. There is no clear evidence, however, that these kinds of remedial approaches lead to more generalized success. Educators, parents, and students understand that being successful requires more than learning isolated facts, developing discrete skills, and obedience to teachers' demands (Kugelmass & Rainforth, 2003).

Systematic instruction, built on behaviorist principles, has certainly provided access to education for many children who would have otherwise languished and who, in the past, were excluded from public schools and communities. However, because these approaches are built on the belief that failure in school is the result of problems within the child, special educators have not traditionally engaged in critical examinations of the learning environments provided in public schools. Special education teachers have not been encouraged to examine the social-political implications of the content and processes of the educational programs they deliver. The relationship between context, culture, social interaction, and learning is largely ignored. This narrow focus has limited the educational experiences of many children and interfered with the development of inclusive schools.

By ignoring the contexts surrounding children's failure, special education has helped sustain an educational system that stigmatizes and oppresses many of the children it was designed to serve.

The field of special education has lacked a critical perspective. Its initial "technicist" orientation reflected a belief that classroom learning was an individual, culturally neutral pursuit (Flinders & Bowers, 1990). Some notable shifts began emerging during the 1990s. Changes in federal legislation and regulations were reflecting a movement away from an exclusive focus on deficit models, reaffirming the importance of educating children alongside typical peers (Individuals with Disabilities Education Act, 1990) and acknowledging the importance of the total learning environment to school success. The success of schoolwide reforms during the late 1980s and early 1990s led the federal government to allow funds granted under Title I of the Elementary and Secondary Education Act (ESEA) to be used for schoolwide programs in addition to direct assistance to individual students (Elementary and Secondary Education Act, 1995). This shift in policy was made in response to the growing understanding of the significance of context to adult expectations for children's learning. Research findings had demonstrated that principals, teachers, and other staff in highly successful schools developed and carried out comprehensive schoolwide reform strategies built on expecting high academic achievement from every child. These schools created safe environments conducive to learning and supported enriched instruction in an expanded core of subjects. Researchers have continued to document that when an entire school is the target of change, even those serving the most disadvantaged youth can succeed (Borman, Hewes, Overman, & Brown, 2003).

These kinds of ESEA Title 1 schoolwide program initiatives supported alternative conceptions of teaching and learning that were also being proposed by some special educators in the 1980s and 1990s (Poplin & Cousin, 1996; Poplin, 1988; Rhodes & Dudley-Marling, 1988; Swadener & Lubeck, 1995). A critical analysis of special schooling was emerging, supported by the understanding that deficit-focused instructional practices and the isolation of students from interactive and collaborative activities contributed to children's learning and social problems (Ainscow, 1999; Berk & Winsler, 1995; Booth & Ainscow, 1998; Skrtic, 1991a, 1991b; Trent, Artiles, & Englert, 1998; Vitello & Mithaug, 1998; Vygotsky, 1978). This understanding reflected a sociocultural perspective central to the development of a social-constructivist curriculum and the movement toward educating children with special educational needs in general education classrooms (i.e., inclusion) during the 1990s.

Skrtic's (1991a, 1991b) theoretical discussions were particularly useful in moving beyond the purely functionalist paradigm that had initially shaped special education. Critical conversations among educators began including an awareness of the importance of the social and political context of schooling on decisions regarding the inclusion of children with disabilities (Bauer & Lynch, 1993; Dyson & Millward, 2000; Franklin, 1994; Kugelmass, 2001; Lipsky & Gartner, 1996; Poplin & Cousin, 1996; Spooner & Johnson, 1996; Swadener & Lubeck, 1995; Trent et al., 1998). A positive relationship between the integration of culturally and individually appropriate instruction with constructivist practices, and the successful inclusion of children with disabilities in general education classrooms were also beginning to be documented (Armstrong, 1993; Bauwens & Hourcade, 1995; Berk & Winsler, 1995; Berres, Ferguson, Knoblock, & Wood, 1996; Campbell, Campbell, & Dickinson, 1996; Mallory & New, 1996; Meyen & Skrtic, 1995; Poplin & Cousin, 1996; Pugach & Johnson, 1995; Stainback & Stainback, 1991, 1996).

Despite evidence of the beginnings of a paradigm shift within special education, support for the exclusion of some children from general education programs continued among both special educators and general education classroom teachers. Many neither understood nor were aware of the limits of research built on medical models that focused on remediation of children's deficits and the assumption that mild disabilities existed as something more than a social construction (Poplin, 1988). Progressive educators, as well as traditionalists, behaviorists, and conservatives, continued to cite this kind of reductionistic research as evidence of the effectiveness of "pull-out" services by specialists or placements in special classrooms and facilities.

Teachers' continued resistance to the inclusion of children with moderate to severe disabilities and other special educational needs in ordinary classrooms can, in part, be explained as an attempt to maintain control within a bureaucratic system that rarely appreciates the complexity of their work (Biklen, 1995; Fullan, 1991; Hargreaves, 1994; Katz, 1971; Sarason, 1996; Weiler, 1988). Teachers are wisely suspicious of nonconsultative, top-down directives. Requiring the inclusion of children who used to be educated elsewhere, without adequate teacher preparation and appropriate support, adds to teachers' workload without offering a clear reward. Teachers also know that they can be penalized for having children in their classrooms who do not do well on standardized tests.

A commitment to ideologies underlying progressive educational practice can also support resistance to including children with special educational needs. The teacher-directed approaches needed by some children to succeed in an *open classroom*, can be perceived as conflicting with the conceptual framework underlying progressive practices (Burman, 1994; Delpit, 1986, 1988; Grumet, 1988; Ladson-Billings, 1994; Mallory &

New, 1996; Rainforth & Kugelmass, 2003). Valerie Walkerdine's (1984) analysis of the historical relationship between child-centeredness and developmental psychology provides insight into what at first seems a paradox, that is, progressive reformers excluding children. Walkerdine describes the ideals of progressive pedagogy and developmental psychology as supporting middle- and upper-class ideologies. The assumption that normal cognitive and psychological development follows predetermined and biologically structured sequential patterns can pathologize children from non-middleclass families and/or nondominant cultures, and others whose learning styles are at variance with dominant culture developmental expectations. Walkerdine's analysis clarifies the ways in which the concept of developmental appropriateness reproduces the theoretical perspective of developmental psychology, validating it and the pedagogies that follow from the assumption that open environments stimulate *all* children's naturally developing capacities. The child who does not respond appropriately to such an environment becomes pathologized.

Although teachers at Betsy Miller describe their instructional approach as child-centered, their ability to successfully integrate a wide range of students in their classrooms required more teacher direction and imposed structure than typically associated with *open education*. In each classroom I observed, social-constructivist practices were adapted to provide culturally and individually appropriate instruction for diverse groups of children. Individualization and direct instruction took place within the context of learning environments that acknowledged and supported differences among children and recognized the importance of social contexts to learning. This kind of eclectic instructional practice is embraced by only a minority of special educators and currently goes against the grain of the agenda for general education reform supported by the federal government. Funding mandates imposed on state departments of education support isolated skill remediation and require standardized testing for all students. These emphases have led more and more teachers to believe that inclusive education is not possible.

A separate special education services delivery system was created in the 1960s and 1970s because, to varying degrees, parents and educators understood that providing an appropriate education for children with special educational needs within the general education system would require a much deeper cultural transformation than seemed possible. Because this separate system focused on deficits within children rather than on radical school reform, it failed to provide the equitable and appropriate educational experiences intended by the federal legislation first enacted in 1975 (Education for All Handicapped Children Act, 1975). The mainstreaming movement of the late 1970s attempted to address some of these inequities.

Unfortunately, as Sarason (1996) points out, mainstreaming failed because it raised "no new questions. It [brought] to the fore old and poorly answered questions" (p. 271).

The failure of earlier attempts to provide public education for all children in "the least restrictive environment," as required by the 1975 Education for All Handicapped Children Act, led to the development of the Regular Education Initiative (REI) in the 1980s. REI proposals recognized that true integration of children with special educational needs required the complete integration of regular and special education systems. Specialized services needed to be provided through collaborative arrangements between educational generalists and specialists. The failure of the REI to reach these goals by the 1990s demonstrates how deeply entrenched the purposes, values, and beliefs that reproduce dominant societal values are in public school systems. As with mainstreaming, the REI proposed reform rather than cultural transformation (Sarason, 1996). Clearly, more than structural changes were needed for the development and sustainability of inclusive schools.

DIMENSIONS OF A CULTURE OF INCLUSION

The story of the Betsy Miller school illustrates one attempt to achieve the kind of cultural transformation needed for the development of an inclusive school. Edward Hall's (1983) three-dimensional model of culture will be used to provide the framework for describing and understanding the school's inclusive culture. Applying Hall's concept of culture will help unravel the complexities surrounding the everyday lives of staff and children and demonstrate the significance of multiple dimensions of school culture. These dimensions are listed in Figure 1.2.

Successful and authentic inclusion requires educational practices designed to support the unique development of each child within general educational settings. These practices develop from direct experience with children rather than strict adherence to external standards, theories, or ideologies. Instructional practices, physical arrangements and artifacts displayed throughout a school and in its classrooms, and the verbal and non-verbal language used by staff represent this visible-technical dimension of a school culture. When asked to reflect on their practice, most teachers can articulate the values and beliefs that underlie these practices. These beliefs represent the second dimension of a school's culture and can also be observed in patterns of interactions seen in the day-to-day life of the school.

Because it operates at unconscious and intuitive levels, teachers

FIGURE 1.2. A Three-Dimensional Model of Culture (Adapted from Hall, 1983)

Dimension I. The visible-technical level observed by insiders and outsiders.

Dimension II. The private level shared by insiders, revealed to trusted outsiders, and seen in patterns of interactions.

Dimension III. The underlying, implicit level of primary culture that links and defines patterns of interconnections between and among each dimension.

---

are generally less aware of the third, implicit dimension of school culture that provides the foundation for their assumptions, beliefs, and actions (Polanyi, 1966). This "hidden dimension" represents the primary level of a culture that can only be revealed by uncovering the "web of interconnections" (Geertz, 1973) that binds each aspect of a culture one to another. Betsy Miller's inclusive culture was held together by a deep appreciation for diversity in all aspects of life and an unconditional love of children. Evidence of this could be seen in teachers' interactions with children and other adults. They were attentive and responsive to the needs of others; negative judgments were absent in their language and action. These kinds of caring relationships reflected a capacity for compassion, that is, the ability to appreciate and understand the suffering of others while seeing their complete humanness, devoid of external expectations or judgments (Dalai Lama & Cutler, 2000; Straub, 2000).

Compassionate caring provides the foundation for inclusive school cultures. These cultures rest on a foundation of what have been described as feminist values and beliefs. Central to these is what Gilligan (1982) refers to as an ethic of care. Rather than being guided by abstract principles, women's decisions and behavior are generally motivated by concerns for social context and relationships. These characteristics can and are seen in men, but are often devalued in institutional life (Antler & Biklen, 1990). Activities associated with caring, such as teaching, are also afforded lower status than those associated with the management and production of goods and services (Freedman, 1990). In spite of social and economic gains by American women during the second half of the twentieth century and, in 2003, growing numbers of women administrators, school systems continue to reflect male domination through the impositions of values and beliefs that contradict those associated with women (Evans, 1995). This dimen-

sion of school culture continues to interfere with the kind of transformation needed for the creation of inclusive schools (Coffey & Delamont,
2000; Halford & Leonard, 2001).

Collaboration: The Visible-Technical Dimension

Given that collaborative instructional practices, schoolwide structures,
and interpersonal interactions have been identified as central to successful
inclusive education (Ainscow, 1999; Bauwens & Hourcade, 1995; Dettmer, Dyck, & Thurston, 1996; Friend & Cook, 1996; Rainforth & York-
Barr, 1997), it is not surprising that collaboration was central to everything
that went on at Betsy Miller. The specific collaborative structures central
to its operation are explored in coming chapters. What will become evident
is that collaborative structures and practices did not exist in a vacuum but
rather were embedded in a deep commitment to compassionate care.

REI proposals for the development of a restructured system, built on
collaborations among professionals, failed because they didn't consider the
complexity of collaboration or the contradictions between values embedded at deeper levels of traditional school cultures and those needed to support a commitment to authentic collaborations. This conflict also reflects
tensions between collaboration, definitions of professionalism, and the his-
toric autonomy of the classroom teacher. Teachers understand that new
directives for change come and go, but school cultures remain, sustained
by classroom teachers. By controlling what goes on in their classrooms,
teachers maintain control of their work. They "take up" the dominant
ideologies of individualism and competition (Weiler, 1998) and remain in
charge of their individual classrooms. Definitions of *professionalism* further project and reinforce images of strong autonomous individuals. The
central role of competition and individualism in American public education
thereby impedes the development of the kinds of collaborative arrangements needed to support inclusive instructional practices (Biklen, 1995;
Fullan & Hargreaves, 1996; Little, 1990; Miller, 1990).

Proposals for including children with special educational needs such as
those developed at Betsy Miller that bring other adults into classrooms as
collaborators threaten teacher autonomy: the possibility of liberation from
isolation is overshadowed by the classroom teacher's prominent sense of
powerlessness within a bureaucratic system. Hargreaves's (1994) investigations of schools identified as collaborative demonstrated that authentic
collaborations among teachers evolved spontaneously and, although supported by institutional leaders such as principals, were generally introduced
by teachers to address initiatives they perceived as important. Their active
participation was voluntary, in response to events as they took place. Col-

laborative activities were primarily informal, outside administratively fixed schedules, and therefore often unpredictable. Although Hargreaves saw the ways collaborations energized teachers and supported needed reforms, he recognized the difficulty of sustaining these kinds of collaborative cultures. "The nonhierarchical, spontaneous, and unpredictable dimensions of these schools were incompatible with school systems where decisions about curriculum and evaluation [were] highly centralized" (p. 193).

Although the number of women in administration is growing, the disproportionately small number of women in leadership positions in public schools (Shakeshaft, 1998) continues to reflect a gendered bias against the kind of collaborative leadership needed in inclusive schools (Kugelmass & Ainscow, 2003). Anderson (1998) points out that although staff participation in school governance may look collaborative, it serves as a "technology of control" (p. 578). When asked to make decisions within a centralized bureaucracy, teachers are often placed in a situation that actually limits their power and authentic decision making. Asking teachers to select instructional approaches to address imposed standards and assure high pass rates on high-stakes tests is one example of this kind of contrivance. Rarely are teachers involved in developing policy or making decisions that lead to authentic reform.

Collegiality: The Private Dimension

Collaboration and *collegiality* are often used interchangeably (Fielding, 1999). In this book, the two are distinguished. Collaborative practices and structures require a collaborative interpersonal style, but collegiality rests on shared commitments to the purpose of the work individuals engage in with one another. Although the two are related and often dependent on each another, it is possible for an individual to go through the motions of a collaborative activity without sharing commitments to its purpose. Promoting collegiality among teachers is, however, central to authentic transformation in schools (Anderson, 1998; Fielding, 1999; Hargreaves, 1982, 1994; Little, 1982; Sergiovanni, 1994) and requires promoting and supporting opportunities for teachers to engage in substantive interchanges and develop trusting relationships.

In traditionally organized schools, teachers generally have limited opportunity to interact with one another. Others set the agenda for their meetings and staff development programs. When teachers do meet with one another, conversations are rarely about what goes on in their classrooms. If teaching is discussed, it generally focuses on gathering "information and assurances" (Little, 1990, p. 513) rather than the exchange of substantive ideas. Not certain if colleagues share their values and beliefs, and fearing criticism, teachers find common ground by talking about families, vacations, entertainment, and everything else except teaching, rather than risk censure or disapproval. Reinforced by the hierarchical structure and authoritarian nature of schools, self-imposed pressures for conformity further limit the quality of teachers' relationships with children, parents, and colleagues and interfere with personal and professional growth. These pressures are often overlooked when trying to understand teachers' disinterest in educational initiatives or continued professional development. Instead, a lack of professional discourse is taken as evidence of anti-intellectualism and reinforces stereotypes of women as passive followers. These negative interpretations support the imposition of top-down directives and teacher training programs that neglect the importance of "connected teaching and learning" (Belenky, Clinchy, Goldberger, & Tarule, 1986). Breaking out of this disempowering cycle has been central to the transformation of Betsy Miller from a traditional to an inclusive culture.

Compassionate Caring: The Primary Dimension

Many teachers of young children become teachers, in part, from a desire to care for children. Traditional school cultures have, however, reinforced and supported a view of caring that does not include compassion but rather requires bringing conformity to children. This definition of *caring for* differs from one in which the needs, desires, and interests of children guide adult interactions (Noddings, 1984). Rather than beginning with openness to the perspectives, desires, and experiences of children, teachers are expected to care for their students by imposing external demands. Grumet (1988) recognizes how a teacher who brings unconditional love and acceptance of children to her classroom may find herself having to subordinate "maternal nurturance" (p. 56) to the demands of the workplace. Even when a teacher believes some demands are inappropriate or not in a child's best interest, school norms push her toward behavioral conformity. Requiring that every child meet the same learning standards at the same time is one such demand, forcing teachers to stigmatize those whose development, learning styles, culture, or ability vary too far from the norm. Caring too much about these children can interfere with doing the job.

Noddings (1984) emphasizes the necessity of resolving this dilemma if authentic inclusion is to be achieved.

> The teacher receives and accepts the student's feeling toward the subject matter; she looks at it and listens to it through his eyes and ears. . . . As she exercises this inclusion, she accepts *his* motives, reaches toward what *he* intends,

as long as these motives and intentions do not force an abandonment of her own ethic. Inclusion as practiced by the teacher is a vital gift. (p. 177)

She believes that teaching represents a "caring relation" only when it is not thought as having a fixed role or following a prescribed set of behaviors (p. 175). No one set of rules or other objective features can be used to describe this kind of relationship.

> Caring involves stepping out of one's personal frame of reference into the other's. When we care we consider the other's point of view, his objective needs, and what he expects of us. . . . Our reason for acting, then, has to do with both the other's wants and desires and the objective elements of his problematic situation. (p. 24)

Compassionate care is only possible in schools where teachers have a good deal of autonomy, flexibility, and support. This brings us back to the importance of collaborative and collegial commitments for creating and sustaining an inclusive school culture.

RESISTANCE TO A CULTURE OF INCLUSION

Given the primacy of caring and significance of relationships in women's development, it seems paradoxical when teachers of young children, most of whom are women, resist the collaborative teaching approaches recommended for inclusive schools and classrooms (Bauwens & Hourcade, 1995; Dettmer et al., 1996; Friend & Cook, 1996; Pugach & Johnson, 1995; Rainforth & York-Barr, 1997; Smith & Scott, 1990). Although these kinds of arrangements could promote the development of a social order where relationships are valued, teachers fear that opening their classrooms to others may mean losing the only autonomy they have in a hierarchical system. Grumet (1988) sees this resistance to collaboration as an example of how women contribute to the continuation of patriarchy:

> At the sound of the bell, she [the teacher] brings the child away from the concrete to the abstract, from the fluid time of the domestic day to the segmented schedule of the school day, from the physical work, comfort, sensuality of home to the mentalistic, passive, sedentary, pretended asexuality of the school—in short, from the woman's world to the man's. She is a traitor, and the low status of the teaching profession may be derived from the contempt her betrayal draws from both sexes. (p. 25)

Carini (2001) believes that teachers' resistance to compassion for and deep understanding of children emerges from a fear of caring too deeply. This kind of resistance limits the nature of the relationships teachers establish with children and further dehumanizes an already dehumanized system.

> Isn't what is being resisted when the child is resisted, the demand the child makes for a fully human and embracing response—a response that is not reducible to grading the child or ranking her or assigning her to a track or some other category? . . . To get to know her so that the school is confronted with her humanness: what she cares about, what she most desires, what gives her utmost satisfaction? (pp. 154–155)

Traditional school cultures support teachers' resistance to collaboration, collegiality, and compassionate caring (Antler & Biklen, 1990; Dorsch, 1998; Muncey & McQuillan, 1996). Ruddick (1980/1999) sees teachers choosing "inauthenticity" in their responses to children as a reflection of an unconscious internalization of the powerlessness they experience within schools (p. 374). Reforms that appear to be supportive of feminist values are resisted in response to the ways power is defined and distributed in schools. Weiler (1988) describes this behavior as evidence of women's attempts to maintain "agency" when operating in disempowering environments. Munro (1998) discusses how women attempt to maintain power and control by "taking up" dominant beliefs, even when they contradict their other values and beliefs:

> Traditionally the rejection of dominant ideologies had constituted "resistance." However, when power is reconceived as not primarily repressive, but as a constellation dispersed within specific micro level contexts, resistance is reduced not merely to opposition but also appropriation of or the taking up of dominant ideologies. (p. 31)

AN EVOLVING RESEARCH DESIGN

Proposals for school reform have ignored both the ways gender is embedded in school cultures and how the nonpredictable nature of much of what takes place within them impacts plans for change. Similarly, the assumptions I initially brought to the research reflected rationally conceived plans and other "grand narratives" (Munro, 1998, p. 28) that ignored the unpredictable nature of what goes on in the "real world" of the children, women, and men at school (Barth, 1990; Muncey & McQuillan, 1996). My constant presence at Betsy Miller reminded me how removed theoretical considerations were from teachers' everyday decisions. Like other feminist researchers (Biklen, 1995; Casey, 1993; Coffey & Delamont, 2000; Grumet, 1998; Luke & Gore, 1992; Munro, 1998; Weiler, 1988; Wolf,

1992), I began to see how reducing the complexity of their lives into a linear historical recounting and an analysis that reflected preexisting theoretical frameworks could diminish teachers' experiences. To resolve this dilemma, during the second year of the research I attempted to engage teachers in a collaborative project that would include their writing about the school. I explained that the intent was not to validate theory, provide definitive answers, or offer a model that could be replicated elsewhere, but rather to offer insight and a sense of connection to other teachers in similar situations. In spite of my frequent attempts to engage teachers in a totally collaborative project, no one was interested. Their passion was teaching, not writing.

My fieldwork began in the fall of 1994 in Karen's second-grade classroom. I became a participant observer once a week for 3 months, and then biweekly, for the remainder of the academic year. I returned the following year, when she moved to a third-grade classroom with the same group of children. That year, I also observed a kindergarten classroom, once a week for 3 months; and a fifth-grade classroom once a week for one month. Each of these three represented one of three grade-level instructional teams (kindergarten and first grade; second & third grade; fourth and fifth grade). In addition to general observations of morning routines, I participated in small-group instruction and assisted children. Less formal observations in several other classrooms were directed at discovering which, if any, features seen in these three classrooms were evident elsewhere. I spoke with children and parents throughout the school, and observed and recorded interactions between adults and children and among children. Material and aesthetic aspects of each classroom visited and the school's two buildings, including architectural design, furniture and seating arrangements, wall decorations, written notices, newsletters, instructional materials, books, toys and games, and so forth were recorded and explained to me by adults and children.

By the end of my first year in Karen's classroom, my research focus began shifting to understanding its relationship to other classrooms. The decision to expand my initial study from individual classrooms to understanding the school's history began at the end of my second year, when the principal, Joe Stefano, transferred to another school. He had been principal at Betsy Miller for 7 years (1987–1995). I wanted to see if and how teachers could sustain the school in the absence of the man identified in the community as its leader. His death the following year heightened my commitment to understanding how a culture built on values and beliefs I shared but rarely found in public schools could be sustained. I also needed to understand how the school came to be as it was.

By the third year of the research, I conducted in-depth, tape-recorded and transcribed interviews with former principals and 10 teachers identified by others as instrumental to the school's evolution. At that point, two teachers I had not interviewed and whose classrooms I had not visited, began to express fears about how my work might be perceived by the "outside world." They, along with one parent, did not want my work to continue. Although I had received permission to conduct the research from school district officials, administrators, teachers, and parents, their concerns triggered a debate among the entire staff.

Discussions with parents and staff became dominated by warlike metaphors. They saw their school being *besieged* by *outside forces*. If my research revealed all the messiness involved in the school's development or publicized problematic issues and debates, I might, it was feared, be giving *ammunition* to *enemies*. These concerns actually were not ungrounded paranoid responses, but reflected growing tensions between the school and the larger school system, centering on a newly imposed districtwide requirement that all elementary schools use a uniform reporting system to document attainment of a uniform set of standards for kindergarten through second-grade students. The new report card reflected a shift in district policy from issues of equity to accountability. Although federal and state regulations continued to mandate racial integration and the inclusion of children with special educational needs in general education settings, newer reforms focused on establishing standards and monitoring student performance. The new superintendent believed that imposing more rigorous standards would compel schools to improve their scores on statewide standardized tests.

Some teachers were concerned that acknowledging the intersecting issues of race, class, gender, assessment, and inclusion at this school could jeopardize its programs. They understood the ways information presented out of context could be used to hurt the school. Teachers at Betsy Miller had seen objective measures (standardized test scores) used to present a skewed image of their school's achievements to the larger community. Some feared that descriptions of everyday behaviors of students, teachers, staff, and parents might similarly be misinterpreted outside the context of the school's culture. These concerns led to the decision not to use the school's real name and remove information that could reveal its identity or that of any individual. The process used in making this decision reflected multiple dimensions of the school's culture. As in other situations, a collaborative decision-making process moderated deeply felt differences among teachers and eventually led to consensus. Participation in the research was to be an individual decision, allowing every teacher to act autonomously, while maintaining a shared commitment to the collaborative decision-making process central to the school's culture. Teachers respected one another's opinions and valued their relationships with colleagues.

Although most teachers at Betsy Miller invited me into their classrooms and openly shared information, I did not have the opportunity to observe every classroom or interview every teacher. To assure the trustworthiness (Lincoln & Guba, 1985) of my interpretations, given the absence of some voices, information from formal interviews was triangulated with less formal discussions with teachers, administrators, parents, and children. Teachers who read drafts of the manuscript agreed that I presented an accurate picture of the school and provided additional feedback for my analysis. This feedback would also include informal conversations with teachers and follow-up interviews with three teachers in 2002. I would also interview school district officials, examine and collect archival materials documenting significant events that took place at the school and in the community from 1983 through 1999, videotape in classrooms, and prepare field notes describing observations of the school.

During the final 2 years of fieldwork (1997–1999), I spent time in the library, playground, and various other settings throughout the school; attended grade-level team meetings, site-based council meetings, parent-child-teacher goal-setting meetings, schoolwide activities; and generally became a familiar face in the school yard and hallways. Themes emerging from the analysis of these collective data were further triangulated with daily routines, organizational structures, and other regulations imposed on the school by outside systems. This analysis revealed the ways feminist values were embedded in multiple levels of the school's culture. Caring relationships among and between administrators, teachers, parents, and children were central to the school's operation. Activities, events, and interactions also reflected the belief that cooperative effort supported individual achievement. The absence of negative judgments in any formal or informal discussions about children illustrated how "maternal nurturance" shaped everyday interactions with children and revealed how deeply it was embedded in the school's culture.

PREVIEW OF BOOK CONTENT

Teachers' responses to children are situated within powerful systems of meaning that shape their practice (Clifford, 1986). These meaning systems can be identified in patterns of everyday behavior and represent several dimensions of culture. This book describes how an inclusive culture evolved at Betsy Miller and how compassionate care supported its teachers in their struggle to sustain their school. Using descriptions of Karen's class-room to illustrate features seen throughout the school, Chapter 2 describes how collaboration, collegiality, and compassionate care were embedded in the school's culture. In Chapters 3, 4, and 5, teachers and administrators instrumental in the school's development examine the school's history. Their stories reveal how maintaining a balance between collaboration and autonomy became central to Betsy Miller's culture. Not only was it necessary for teachers to maintain a positive tension between individual and group needs in their work with children and while working with other adults, but it would also become central to negotiating new demands imposed on the school by the school district's central administration.

The exploration of the school's evolution continues in Chapter 6, focusing on teachers' and parents' responses to a directive from the district superintendent requiring every elementary school to use a uniform, skills-based, developmental checklist as the report card for all first and second graders. This requirement challenged the assessment and reporting system that had been developed by teachers at Betsy Miller, just when their principal of 7 years transferred to another school and priorities in state and national educational reforms were shifting from equity to accountability. These events provided an unanticipated opportunity to examine the sustainability of this school's culture in the absence of a supportive principal. This chapter explores how teachers joined parents to negotiate with the school district administration and maintain their own assessment process. To do this, they called on collaborative processes and leadership skills developed during their participation in the school's evolution. This story provides one example of a heroic struggle by teachers committed to promoting social justice in the face of demands for greater uniformity in public education and the promotion of corporate models of organization and management.

Chapter 7 provides an examination of the implications of this school's evolution for sustaining school cultures built on collaboration, collegiality, and compassionate care in an increasingly bureaucratized and politicized educational system. The need for teachers and administrators who are skillful at collaboration, compromise, and resistance is emphasized; suggestions for the preparation and ongoing development of teachers are offered, and existing conceptions of leadership are challenged through a comparative analysis of leadership at Betsy Miller and two inclusive schools in England. The chapter concludes by pointing out that although those most directly affected by what goes on in schools (teachers, parents, and children) appear to have the least power, they will ultimately determine whether or not progressive educational reform can be sustained in the twenty-first century.

CHAPTER 2

A Culture of Inclusion

Each time I talked with teachers from Betsy Miller, I became more intrigued. They always spoke positively about children and described their school as both an "inclusive community" and "bias-free zone." I was particularly interested in gaining a deeper understanding of how these teachers organized and operated classrooms and thought about what they did. Little did I suspect that my visit to their school one morning in early October 1994 would grow into a project designed to investigate the relationship between deep levels of culture and the ability to create and sustain an inclusive school. I came to Karen Shriver's classroom that day to learn more about her teaching, but soon would want to know more about how the entire school had eliminated pull-out services for special education, Title 1 reading and math, and English as a Second Language (ESL).

The exclusion of those whose learning styles, interests, and intelligences didn't match the requirements of a mandated curriculum and whose behavior didn't conform to definitions of *appropriateness* relieved pressure on teachers. Excluding these children also allowed business to go on as usual though it wasn't necessarily best for the children. Although special education and other remedial programs delivered in separate settings might improve the academic skills of some students, this kind of instructional arrangement limited social interactions with abler peers. In my work with both general and special education teachers, I found that although most teachers understood this and were interested in moving toward implementing practices that supported greater diversity in their classrooms, many faced obstacles they were unable or unwilling to challenge. While some teachers focused on children's problems, pathologizing their behavior and hoping a referral to special education would lead to medication or removal from their classroom, others were genuinely interested in examining and changing their own practice in order to more effectively support every child. Traditional curriculum, high-stakes standardized tests, rigid structures, centralized bureaucracies, and inflexible special education regulations were, however, often insurmountable barriers. Many teachers also saw themselves as powerless and unable to voice the ideas that drove their desire to change. Those who made the enormous leap over and beyond internal and systemic barriers often confronted collegial rivalry, student and parent resistance, and the difficulty of balancing the demands of professional, personal, and family life. I wanted to know if and how Karen and other teachers at Betsy Miller had overcome these obstacles.

THE ANNEX

The first time I visited Karen's second-grade classroom, I couldn't find her. Standing in the doorway of the room, I scanned the heads of 8- and 9-year-olds, looking for an adult's. Two appeared, but neither was hers. I was sure this was the right room. Karen's photograph was taped to one of the 12 construction paper birthday cakes tacked along the border of one wall, along with those of children and two other White women. I had entered the Betsy Miller Annex as instructed, through the side door that led to the large open space at the center of the building and signed in with the librarian sitting amidst a jumble of children's books and papers, surrounded by walls with even more books. She had directed me to this classroom.

I had been in the building before, but had never really paid attention to the bright colors and light of the large open space that served as its hub. As I looked around, the institutional feeling of the somewhat cold gray stone and stucco exterior facade of this one-story building began fading. Built in 1969, it faced the older, three-story, red brick main school building across the street, and was designated as the early childhood center. Young children and adults sat around tables filled with children's books, reading and talking softly with one another. That October morning, it housed six prekindergarten through first-grade classrooms and Karen's second-grade class. The other second-grade class had moved to the larger building across the street, but Karen had asked to remain there and keep the same group she had been with the year before in first grade. Her request had been granted even though it meant separating her class from the other second-grade class. It would also mean that meetings with other teachers on the same instructional team would be less convenient. These teams met once a week and were organized by grade level: kindergarten and Grade 1; Grades 2 and 3; Grades 4 and 5. Granting Karen's request to stay at the Annex with this group of children went against structural norms, but reflected a more central aspect of the school's culture: Staff decisions here were guided by what teachers and administrators considered "best for kids."

Because of staffing changes, Karen had only been with her current group of children for one year. Teachers generally stayed with the same children for 2 years, through a process called *looping*. Believing strongly that continuity was important for young children, given the discontinuity many experienced in their lives, Karen asked to stay with this group for another year. By staying together and remaining at the Annex, the three children in the classroom who were classified as learning disabled and/or emotionally disturbed would not have to learn a new routine, in a new space, with different teachers. All of the students would be familiar with Karen and one another, the norms of the classroom, the routine and physical setup of the Annex. She hoped this would help maintain the rhythm they had built during their first year together and minimize the difficulties some students experienced with transitions. Staying together would also maximize the sense of community Karen believed to be central to the success of her classroom. It was, she felt, worth the inconvenience of walking across the street to meet with other teachers.

The Annex's identity as the school's early childhood center supported a more open and relaxed ambiance than elementary school buildings serving older students. Its physical layout was different from the typical "egg-carton" structure that reinforced the isolation of teachers and students (Spillane, Halverson, & Diamond, 2001). The building's design reflected the open-space concept promoted by progressive school architects during the 1960s and 1970s. The large open space I had entered was designed to be its hub, and served as the library and resource center for teachers and students. What I saw that morning, however, represented a modification of the Annex's original design. When first constructed, no walls divided the interior space from individual classrooms. Instead, students met with teachers in clusters at the perimeter of the central hub. This arrangement was meant to provide easy and equal access to all individuals, resources, and facilities, and thereby promote collaboration.

Architectural innovation did not translate easily, however, into educational practice. Because most teachers and students experienced the large open-space design as distracting, partitions were built, creating separate classrooms. These walls resembled spokes emanating from the Annex's central hub. Walls and a door closed off some classrooms, like Karen's—while others remained partially opened. I would eventually come to see this modification of the open-school concept as a metaphor for the ways in which ideologically based practices were continually examined and modified at Betsy Miller in response to the individual needs, interests and abilities of students and teachers, as well as to demands emanating from outside its walls. The variety of classroom spaces here reflected teachers' understanding that social environments needed to consider both collective and individual needs. My visit to Karen's classroom would provide a first glimpse into these aspects of the school's culture.

KAREN'S CLASSROOM

The librarian had directed me to a room at the end of one of the spokes, closed off from the center space by two walls. Twenty-three yellow stars, each with the name of a child or adult, including Karen, invited visitors into the "Star Room." I may have been looking for her classroom but, as the name on the door indicated, it had a more collective identity. Inside, fluorescent lights from the central hub were visible through the upper glass section of the wall to the right of the door where multicolored wall hangings, resembling large versions of the pot holders kids weave at camp were hung. Twenty-six $8\frac{1}{2} \times 11$ inch laminated cards, each with a handwritten upper- and lower-case letter of the alphabet framed two other walls. Children's illustrations of objects or actions, and words that began with the indicated letter hung above each. Multicolored plastic bins holding children's books were stacked on rows of shelves lining the wall to the left of the door, beneath windows that ran the length of the room. An angular, wooden room divider displaying more books jutted out at a right angle halfway along this wall, creating a reading corner where two children curled up on soft pillows, reading. Beyond the bookcase divider, three more worked on Macintosh computers. Two others sat alone, working at desks.

The room hummed with children's energy, somewhat restrained within the container of a classroom. Nonetheless, they seemed relaxed, engaged with one another and their work. Sitting in groups of three or four, in pairs, or alone, none of these 20 girls and boys took notice as this middle-aged White woman entered their world. Only a few looked up from their work, but even they returned quickly to the more interesting things at their desks. In addition to children from the surrounding, predominantly White, middle- to upper-middle-class neighborhood, these students included children from international families affiliated with the nearby university, and others bused from "downtown," where the majority of African American, Latino, and Asian refugee families lived. There were an equal number of girls and boys here. Half were White, and the rest represented a mix of African American, Asian, and Latino children. I would later learn that English was the second language for 5 of these children. I already knew that at least 3 others had been classified as being in need of special education.

Continuing to glance around the room, I noticed that except for photographs of animals, a poster of Martin Luther King, a map of Africa, and an American flag, the room was decorated exclusively with children's work or charts explaining assignments. Their drawings and written remarks about a story they had read hung on one wall. Illustrated and word-processed poetry was tacked to a large bulletin board on another wall above the three Macintosh computers. I was struck by the range of topics and varied levels of sophistication of their poetry.

As I walked toward one of the two women seated among a cluster of children, I felt somewhat anxious, disappointed, and a bit annoyed that Karen wasn't there. One woman was a student teacher from the nearby university, the other a parent volunteer. They explained that Karen had gone to telephone a parent, would be back shortly, and invited me to join the children. I decided to sit at a table with two boys and two girls, each doing something different: two reading books at very different levels of difficulty, one writing a book report, and the fourth working on a rough draft of a storybook she was writing. The two working on writing assignments had purple and blue folders, while the others had blue ones. I had seen children take folders like these from a large box in the center of the room. The four children explained that the blue ones were for reading and the purple for writing assignments. When I asked if everyone's was the same, one boy remarked, "Sure, they're all blue and purple." It was only after looking inside that I discovered the folders held different assignments, geared to the abilities, interests, and needs of each child. Indeed, as the boy had suggested, some assignments were the same, but others were quite different. All were designed to reinforce specific skills and concepts and provide reminders of activities and ongoing projects students could engage in throughout the day. When asked why some children had different assignments than others, the same boy responded quite matter-of-factly, "Everyone always does different things." My question seemed strange to a child whose only school experiences had been at Betsy Miller.

Karen returned a few minutes later. Apologizing, she explained that a child had been out sick for several days, and she needed to speak with his mother. When I responded with surprise at the independence of the children, particularly so early in the year, she laughed. "I take their independence for granted, I guess. It's what I expect and is central to everything that goes on here. They shouldn't need me around all the time. They have a lot of choice in the work they do, and they usually challenge themselves. If they have a problem, they can ask each other or one of the other adults or do something else in the room till they can get assistance on something they are stuck on. They all know what they can do." My first visit had been only 6 weeks into the school year, and yet every child clearly knew what was expected. There was certainly a sense of order in the classroom and it seemed to require minimal external control and vigilance. The fact that it was the students' second year with Karen certainly helped.

Curriculum and Instruction

I would continue visiting Karen's classroom twice a month throughout the year and into the next, when she moved with the same group of children to the main building across the street. During these visits, I videotaped interactions among children and between teachers and students, spoke with children, and participated in whole-class lessons. Through these conversations, interactions, and observations, I came to understand how this classroom worked, and discovered intrinsic values and beliefs embedded in its operation. Moving to the older, three-story school building the following year would not significantly alter children's interactions or instructional processes. In both settings, an environment would be created where differences in culture, social class, temperament, learning styles, interests, and abilities were accommodated to allow for individual variation in performance within group activities. Karen believed that assignments that were "close-ended"—that is, could be completed only in one way and had only one correct outcome—excluded some children from participation. This kind of social exclusion interfered with developing autonomy and competence as well as the sense of belonging she believed essential for creating a welcoming and productive classroom community. Authentic participation required more than having every child do the same thing as everyone else.

Karen's instructional practices were designed to create what she and others at the school referred to as "multiple entry points." All assignments and activities needed to both challenge and support the successful participation of every child. Karen achieved this by designing whole-class activities that allowed for differentiation. For example, when a fictional story or factual lesson was presented, the method of presentation would consider the relationship of the content to children's experiences as well as the language ability and learning styles of each student. Opening up the curriculum also meant providing children with varied means of expression. For verbal literacy, this meant some children would compose their own storybooks, while others wrote sentences, lists, or single words, accompanied by pictures or drawings. Regardless of skill level, all the children were expected to share their written work with classmates, who would ask questions, offer positive feedback, and make suggestions for improvement. In mathematics, opening up meant accepting, supporting, and critiquing the different methods children used for solving problems.

I would later learn that although every teacher at Betsy Miller accommodated student diversity somewhat differently, every classroom approached instruction in ways that made the curriculum accessible to all students.

Individual needs and strengths were considered in designing group lessons and activities. These approaches adapted progressive, learner-centered, constructivist models that included whole language approaches to literacy, writers' and readers' workshops, student-generated projects and thematic units, and hands-on, conceptual mathematics.

Planning and Support

All of this required a good deal of planning and preparation that was rarely done by only one teacher. Karen and every other *lead teacher* had the support of additional adults in their classrooms. Lead teachers were certified in elementary education. They stayed with the same group of children throughout the day and remained with them for 2 years (looping). Other adults in the room were identified as either *professional collaborators* or *classroom collaborators*. Professional collaborators were certified in special education, speech and language therapy, English as a second language, or remedial reading or math; they spent half days in two classrooms from the same instructional team (kindergarten-first; second-third; fourth-fifth). Classroom collaborators were paraprofessionals who were not certified as teachers: They held full-time assignments in one classroom. The professional collaborator in Karen's room was a remedial math teacher who shared teaching responsibilities there every afternoon, and in another second-grade class in the morning. She planned, organized, and conducted whole-class math lessons, cotaught other subjects with Karen, and assisted children with individual work. Having another adult in the class for half of each day supported individualization, accommodating a wide range of student abilities and skills.

Karen's classroom reflected her unique teaching style and the values and beliefs she brought to her work, but many aspects of her classroom were influenced by outside decisions. To better understand the relationship between her classroom and the rest of the school, I began speaking with other teachers, support staff, and administrators. It soon became apparent that what I saw in Karen's classroom was not unique. To discover more about how other classrooms resembled hers, I began observing others. During the second year, I spent more time at the school talking with other teachers, students, and administrators, and observing and recording interactions between adults and children and among children in the library, playground, and other settings. I became a participant observer in two other classrooms as well as Karen's, a kindergarten and a fourth-grade class—each of the three classes represented one of the grade-level teams. I attended grade-level team meetings and schoolwide events, and had casual conversations with teachers and children in the hallways. This collective information would be used to capture the school's culture.

A SCHOOLWIDE CULTURE OF INCLUSION

A mission statement was prominently displayed in every school I visited in the United States during the late 1980s and early 1990s. Betsy Miller was no exception. Its mission statement was adopted in 1993:

MISSION STATEMENT

Whereas the Betsy Miller staff has undergone an extensive needs assessment of our school and has identified important elements that will strengthen our school environment, be it resolved that we commit ourselves to maximizing instructional outcomes for culturally diverse students. Recognizing that education is the cornerstone of democracy, our charge is to foster the way into a larger society. By acceptance, accommodation, and especially affirmation of cultural diversity, we believe students and staff will be empowered to succeed.

Three interrelated principles were also identified by the staff to articulate the philosophy guiding their school:

1. *Purpose:* School is for children.
2. *Value:* Inclusion.
3. *Belief:* All children can succeed; diversity is enriching; families are central.

Knowing that publicly articulated beliefs rarely reflect what goes on inside classrooms, I initially noted these statements as interesting artifacts. After 2 years of observation and interaction with staff and children, my initial skepticism began fading. Instructional practices and organizational structures at Betsy Miller actually operationalized these ideals. In the following sections, themes that emerged from data gathered through fieldwork and document analysis are organized by applying Edward Hall's three-dimensional model of culture (see Chap. 1 and Fig. 1.2). This analysis demonstrates the relationship between visible features and deeper levels of the school's culture. Revealing their interconnections (Geertz, 1973) will provide an understanding of the meaning of a *culture of inclusion.*

The Visible-Technical Dimension: Collaboration

Although the visible-technical dimension of a culture may be the easiest to understand, it is often the most difficult to describe completely. It includes everything: all material objects, physical space and the ways in which they are used; language usage; people and their interactions with one another; assessment and instructional methods and materials; scheduling and the allocation of time. Rather than trying to re-create every artifact and encounter, I will give an analysis of those visible aspects of the school that were consistently observed across classrooms and described by teachers as supporting diversity among students.

Students in every classroom included nonnative speakers of English, those identified as having special educational needs, and others whose knowledge and skills exceeded expectations for children of their age. There was constant and continual collaboration among teachers and the diverse groups of children in their classrooms. These interactions were embedded in everything that went on there: in how teachers talked and organized lessons, and in the models they provided children through their interactions with one another. Although a good deal of thought and planning had gone into what I observed in classrooms, these interactions appeared natural and reflected what Friend and Cook (1996) describe as a "collaborative interpersonal style." Figure 2.1 summarizes the characteristics of these kinds of interactions.

Adults and children appeared to be working voluntarily with one another, as equals. During classroom activities, adults shared responsibility for participation and accessing resources, and appeared equally accountable. Describing interactions at Betsy Miller as collaborative does not, however, fully capture the quality of what went on there. Individuality and autonomy were also important. Collaborations were not only concerned with group interests, but balanced collective and individual concerns. For

FIGURE 2.1. Characteristics of a Collaborative Interpersonal Style (Adapted from Friend & Cook, 1996)

- Voluntary
- Parity among participants
- Collective ownership of goals
- Shared responsibility for participation and decision making
- Sharing of resources and knowledge
- Shared accountability for outcomes

teachers, this meant operating classrooms in ways that reflected their unique approaches to instruction and classroom management, while maintaining collective commitments to colleagues. For students, this meant individual needs and interests were acknowledged and accommodated within group activities. Balancing group and individual desires was essential for empowering and supporting teachers' skills and creativity and supporting children with very diverse needs, interests, and abilities in the same classroom.

Classroom practices and schoolwide structures consistently identified as central to the operation of the school and observed across classrooms in both the Annex and main building are listed in Figure 2.2.

Instructional Practices. Curriculum and instruction varied somewhat across classrooms, but shared many of the same features as in Karen's classroom. Throughout the school, a progressively oriented, constructivist curriculum was tempered by a commitment to assuring that instruction was culturally relevant and individually appropriate for every child. Flexibility, individualization, and concerns for equity pervaded the content and process of teaching in every classroom observed. Aesthetic arrangements included displays of children's work, of celebrating achievements, and of promoting cross-cultural awareness. Classwide projects were common and the arts were integrated into every classroom. Student's written and artistic achieve-

FIGURE 2.2. Classroom Practices and Schoolwide Structures at Betsy Miller

Classroom Practices

Constructivist curriculum
Narrative assessment process
Collaborative teaching
Cooperative learning
Immersion for English as a Second
  Language
Conflict management
Flexible seating among students
Student-focused aesthetics
Lunch with teachers
Focus on cultural diversity

Schoolwide Structures

Blended services
Grade-level instructional teams
Looping
Site-based council

ments were hung on classroom walls; themes and images related to diversity were displayed everywhere.

ESL teachers worked with classroom teachers to adapt instruction and support individual students with limited proficiency in English. Some worked as collaborators while others served as support teacher for several classrooms. At times, small groups of children would participate in a language *immersion* experience with an ESL support teacher. These children worked on specific activities before they were introduced to the entire class. The ESL teacher introduced relevant vocabulary and concepts identified in collaboration with the classroom teacher. This enabled children with limited English vocabulary to participate successfully in the same activities as their peers and, at times, take a leadership role in the classroom. The ESL teacher would come into the room, and participate in the activity alongside other classroom teachers.

The Narrative Assessment Process. Children's work was not compared to external standards. Neither evaluative grades nor grade levels were assigned. Rather, assessment began by understanding and describing each child in great detail. This process was initiated at a collaborative goal setting conference held early in the school year. The lead teacher and, when appropriate, other staff would meet with every parent or caregiver and child to identify what each believed should be achieved in the coming year. Children and parents or other caregivers presented their goals to teachers, who explained academic and social-emotional expectations. Teachers then combined information from observations of the child's learning and behavior and examples of the child's work gathered in a portfolio with the goals identified during these discussions, creating a baseline for monitoring children's progress. Each child's progress would be reported to parents through narrative assessment reports written midterm and summarized at the end of the school year.

Establishing goals with parents or caregivers and students supported authentic collaboration with families. This was particularly important for engaging grandparents, relatives, foster parents, single parents, non-English speakers, ethnic or racial minorities, and refugee families. Flexible arrangements were made to assure that teachers met with every caregiver. The broad base of parental support for the narrative assessment process would become obvious later in the research when the school district questioned the value and appropriateness of this kind of student-centered assessment. Parental support would help sustain this practice. All parents I spoke with emphasized how the narrative assessment process demonstrated teachers' deep understanding and unconditional respect for their child. Quakie Onaygo, an African American teacher with close ties to the local community, believes this process was central to establishing collaborative relationships between teachers and African American families. As Quakie told me, "Parents say, 'My, you know my kid. No one has ever gone into such detail and depth about knowing who my kid is.'"

Parents were rarely mentioned in most of my conversations with teachers. This may have been a consequence of my initial research focus on classroom instructional practice. The questions I asked elicited responses that limited my understanding of the ways parents and other family members were or were not included in the life of the school. I knew there was an open-door policy, inviting family members to stop by anytime. When they did, teachers appeared relaxed and welcoming. Parent volunteers frequently participated in classroom activities. However, in spite of genuine attempts by teachers and administrators to get a broader representation, family involvement in the PTA and other parent volunteer programs remained dominated by middle-class parents.

Classroom Management. Every room had flexible seating arrangements that changed with different activities. During whole-class lessons or class meetings, children sat in a circle, on chairs or on the floor. When working on individual lessons and activities, they sat in clusters or pairs and, although there were occasions when they worked on their own, most worked with one another. Although clearly organized around instruction, classrooms were rarely quiet places. Children were actively engaged in both individual work and group activities. While most teachers used informal strategies such as conversations about supporting one another and drawing children's attention to the significance of cooperation in the stories they read, others used more structured approaches to cooperative learning.

Conflict management strategies were taught to children. Teachers guided discussions to include problem-solving strategies whenever the agenda of a class meeting focused on interpersonal conflicts in and outside the classroom. I never witnessed physical aggression between children, nor angry interchanges with teachers. If a child seemed disinterested in participating in a whole-class or group activity, an adult might engage the child in a discussion or ignore the behavior. Teachers' strategies depended on the individual child but consistent nonparticipation would lead to rethinking the activity. During 9 years of my unannounced as well as anticipated visits to the school, I never witnessed coercion, humiliation, or harsh punishment.

Classrooms were responsive to the individual needs and interests of children, rather than focused on control and conformity. The narrative assessment process deepened teachers' understanding of each child and family and helped establish a comfortable classroom environment for every child. The content and process of what went on there considered race, class, gender, and linguistic differences to create what teachers described as "culturally responsive classrooms." Whenever possible, at least two children who spoke the same language, shared the same racial or ethnic backgrounds, or came from similarly nontraditional families, such as having gay or lesbian parents or being raised by grandparents or other nonparental caregivers, were "clustered" in the same classroom. Teachers believed this helped relieve a sense of isolation among minority children.

Teachers worked to develop strong, positive relationships with children. They were equally concerned with the children's relationship with peers and establishing a sense of a classroom community. Teachers consistently mentioned the schoolwide practice of eating lunch in the classroom with children every day as supporting this development. Quakie said, "It's such an important time to build a sense of community by breaking bread together. It's that time to get that one-on-one with that particular kid that you knew missed something that morning. Just the whole eating together, cements the family feel of the classroom."

Schoolwide Structures. The other seven elementary schools in this small northeastern city did not, in 1994, provide support in general education classrooms for children with disabilities and those receiving services through Title 1 programs. Rather, children were pulled out to receive individual support services from special educators, remedial teachers, or related services providers (i.e., occupational therapists, physical therapists, speech and language pathologists, counselors, psychologists, and social workers). Students considered to have more intense needs were placed in separate special education classrooms and mainstreamed into general education classrooms or special subject classes (art, music, physical education) when considered appropriate. Non-English speakers were removed from general education classrooms to receive instruction in English as a second language.

Rather than being assigned to individual children, support personnel at Betsy Miller were attached to grade-level instructional teams and collaborated with classroom teachers. These individuals were not publicly identified by specific discipline, certification area, or title, but were known as either *professional collaborators* or *classroom collaborators*. Professional collaborators were certified teachers, and classroom collaborators were paraprofessionals. This schoolwide support system was called *blended services*. Figure 2.3 illustrates the central role of this organizational structure in supporting classroom practices, showing how each was embedded in a shared understanding of the school's purpose, values, and beliefs.

The principal, in collaboration with instructional teams, decided which adults went where. These decisions were based on matching needs and

FIGURE 2.3. Blended Services Embedded in a Schoolwide Philosophy

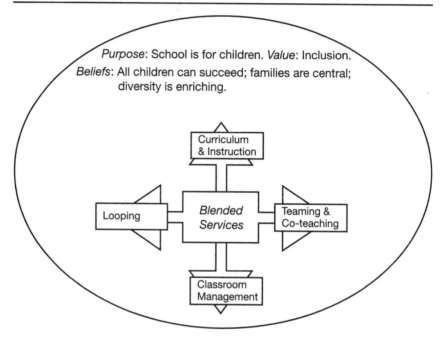

abilities of children with the experience and expertise of the lead teachers—some of whom were certified in special education as well as elementary education—and the support personnel available. Decisions by the school district regarding the number of paraprofessionals and support staff, as well as the specific qualifications of the professional staff assigned to the school, depended on the total number of children falling within the designated poverty range and those identified as eligible for special education, remedial reading or math, speech and language therapy, and English as a second language. Because there were not enough specialists at the school to work in every classroom, or even be part of each instructional team, some were designated as *support teachers*. These teachers consulted with instructional teams, worked with individual children and provided additional support in classrooms. For example, although Karen had three children identified as eligible for special education, her collaborator was a math teacher. That year, she would call on the special education support teacher for consultations regarding individual children. A few years later, this system would change to provide scheduled consultation for all teachers who had students classified for special education.

The school district's Committee on Special Education assigned individ-

ual aides to students identified as having extensive management needs—
that is, children who were deaf, autistic or had severe physical impairments
or severe behavior problems. In these instances, staff decisions regarding
the placement of a child also meant deciding which classroom grouping
would be best served by having an additional full-time aide. Instructional
teams made recommendations regarding the placement of children in classrooms, and submitted these decisions to the principal for approval. These
decisions were based on information about individual students and which
teachers worked best with which children. Children with high-level special
educational needs were occasionally clustered in classrooms where special education teachers were assigned as collaborators and a full-time aide
was assigned; the number of children with special educational needs in a
classroom was limited to four, depending on the nature of their needs and
whether an individual aide was assigned to provide additional support.

These considerations further complicated decisions regarding children's placement in classrooms. Staff collaboration was vital to creating
classroom groupings. Teachers and collaborators voiced preferences for
which children they felt prepared to teach and the adults they wanted to
work with. They would be staying with the same group of children and
working with one another for 2 years. Teachers believed looping children
and staff helped classroom teams develop effective teaching and management strategies and create what was often referred to as a "classroom community." At the end of the second year with the classroom teaching team,
children would move to another classroom for the next 2 years, while their
former teachers would begin again, with a younger group of children. Everyone agreed that this arrangement supported the development of strong
interpersonal relationships with children and families.

The knowledge, skills, and experiences of teachers, collaborators,
and the staff were central to creating classroom teams with adults whose
skills, approaches to teaching, and temperament complemented one another. Once classroom groupings were formed, decisions regarding which
adults worked with which children were made collectively by each classroom team, as were decisions regarding daily schedules and classroom
management. Although lead teachers did not take sole responsibility for
these decisions or for carrying out instruction, differences in education,
years of experience, and their desire for some degree of professional autonomy made them positional leaders of their classroom team.

Paraprofessionals were neither involved in setting goals for students
nor held as accountable for children's performance as were certified teachers or professional collaborators. Paid an hourly wage, classroom collaborators and aides were not required to attend grade-level team planning
sessions, parent conferences, staff development programs, or other after-

school meetings. Conflicts related to differences in status and pay among lead teachers, professional collaborators, and paraprofessionals would emerge as I spent more time at the school. The ways professional and non-professional staff interacted publicly masked these status differentiations and hid conflicts from outsiders. Their differences included more than salary, educational background, and professional preparation. Social class, race, language, and ethnicity also divided the staff. Teachers, professional collaborators, and specialists were primarily White, middle-class women, while "paras" had less education, lower incomes, and included more non-Whites and non-English speakers.

The Private Dimension: Collegiality

This level of culture is revealed to only a select few and generally denied to outsiders. Although individuals observing specific practices may not be aware of the invisible standards guiding the way a school operates, insiders understand and can articulate this second dimension of culture. Teachers at Betsy Miller consistently described the classroom practices and structural arrangements found at the visible level of its culture as supporting their belief in inclusion. Rather than relating this concept only to individuals with disabilities, *inclusion* and *exclusion* were understood in terms of social marginalization in general. This definition differed from that used by the school district. The district's intent was to provide additional, remedial support for individual children. At Betsy Miller all teachers were seen as teachers of all children, as collaborative teachers rather than remediators or specialists.

These differences were reflected in limited referrals for special education by teachers at Betsy Miller. Referrals were rarely, if ever, made during kindergarten or first grade for children exhibiting learning and/or behavior problems. Teachers wanted to avoid the classification systems used by the state and school district that they believed stigmatized children and set in motion a cycle of lowered expectation. Teachers were particularly reluctant to refer children of color to the school district's Committee on Special Education. They knew that a disproportionate number of African American boys were referred for special education services and left school before graduation at higher rates than Whites. Betsy Miller teachers also understood that their decision to not refer children would result in receiving fewer support personnel from the school district but believed it a worthwhile sacrifice. They also believed that the environments provided in their classrooms were appropriate for all children and feared that a special education referral would lead to placing a child in a segregated special education facility.

The lack of referrals for special education reflected their awareness and concern regarding institutional racism. The staff had declared their school a bias-free zone. Teachers had become aware of the ways in which racism and other forms of oppression were embedded in everyday interactions and language. Their heightened awareness was heard in discussions among adults and children, and seen in reading materials, posters, and wall decorations in classrooms and throughout the schools. Teachers discussed their personal commitments to combating racial, cultural, religious, and gender discrimination with children. Gender-neutral and nonstereotypical language was taught, modeled, and reinforced. Gender inequities were pointed out and deliberately countered by actively encouraging children to participate in non-gender-stereotypical activities—such as teaching boys to knit and encouraging girls to join coed baseball and soccer leagues. Cooperation was more valued than competition. Noncompetitive games and activities were developed and encouraged, as was praise for doing one's personal best.

There was a strong feminist consciousness among teachers. They identified hierarchical administrative structures and authoritarian decision-making processes as representing oppressive male models. Clearly, Betsy Miller was not operating in the typical hierarchical fashion that reflected an underlying belief in authoritarian control that dominates public education. Rather, its operation seemed similar to other schools that have been described as collegial, learning communities (Dorsch, 1998; Hargreaves, 1982; Henry, 1996; Little, 1982; Miller, 1990; Pounder, 1998; Sergiovanni, 1994; Smith & Scott, 1990).

Staff saw the collaborative arrangements that characterized their school as a vehicle for achieving their antibias agenda. They also acknowledged how difficulties, longstanding concerns, and conflicts among them could impact on their collaborations. Conflicts existed but were not obvious to most outsiders. These included tensions between certified teachers and noncredentialed staff, who worked at lower salary levels, with or without benefits. Teachers advocated for pay raises and increased benefits for nonprofessional staff and supported the formation of a union for paraprofessionals. They also understood how inequities in power and status among the staff reflected societal inequities. This reflected their recognition of how schools and classrooms were sites that mirrored the "culture of power" of the larger society (Delpit, 1988). The nonprofessional staff understood that teachers were not responsible for their lower pay and appreciated teachers' support during salary negotiations. Putting children at the center of their work allowed individual concerns of to be balanced by the collective needs of the classroom.

Sandy Walden, a European American teacher who came to Betsy Miller in 1983, described the way staff resolved their differences:

We may disagree, but it really is within some general assumption of a multicultural education; a curriculum that's open-ended, that is inclusive, that allows all children to succeed within that program. So when we argue, there's a great sense of respect for one another, and often you'll hear people put ideas out—they just sort of put ideas out and say, "I'm thinking out loud, I'm trying this out, I want to hear what you have to say." Other people's ideas are honestly as important as their own, because we all understand clearly now that any individual idea isn't so great anymore, but when we all put our heads together we come up with something.

The decision to put on a public face of congeniality did not reflect what Hargreaves (1994) refers to as "contrived collegiality." Rather, it represented shared acknowledgment of vulnerability. The staff knew that although they were empowered to make decisions within the school, they had only limited power in relation to the larger school system. Some of the practices central to the school's culture were inconsistent with school district policy and state regulations. This led to a heightened sense of vulnerability among teachers that became evident in the military metaphors used during discussions about the relationship between the school and the school district. Teachers saw themselves as *bombarded* by outside *forces* and needed to make sure the *enemy* didn't use internal disputes as *ammunition*.

The principal, Joe Stefano, was the *advance guard*, standing between the school and the school district's central administrative offices. Teachers knew that he shared their commitments and beliefs, and would support any decision based on what was best for kids. His advocacy for the blended services model was central to the school's development and its teachers' ability to sustain their commitment to inclusion. His negotiations with the school district for support services and additional resources needed to include evidence that the services indicated in children's Individual Education Plans (IEP) were being provided. In spite of his skilled negotiations, conflicting beliefs regarding the identification of children needing special education services would continue to limit the number and qualifications of personnel assigned to the school, threatening the sustainability of its culture.

The Primary Dimension: Compassionate Caring

The values and beliefs that exist at this level are the foundation of a culture. Because they operate at unconscious and intuitive levels, teachers are often unaware of how primary level assumptions are reflected in the way a school operates. Uncovering implicit beliefs is, however, essential to understanding the interconnections that ultimately constitute a school's culture. At Betsy Miller, an unconditional acceptance of children provided the foundation for practices that reflected the values and beliefs articulated by the staff.

Caring for children was the center of adult agendas. This could be seen in interactions between staff and children. Adult language was devoid of references to deficits or labels. Teachers worked with one another to support children in ways that were qualitatively different from team-teaching arrangements I had seen elsewhere. Although hierarchical roles officially existed at Betsy Miller, differentiating lead teachers from professional and classroom collaborators and other support staff, these roles were not apparent to either outsider observers or children. This blurring of formal roles reflected Noddings (1984) belief that only when teaching is not thought of as assuming a role or following a prescribed set of behaviors can it become a caring relationship. Every adult anticipated what needed to be done; assisted one another, shared professional expertise and personal knowledge, and took responsibility for any child. Children approached one another or any available adult, including me, asking for help. At times, a teacher or collaborator might work with an individual child on a specific activity or skill that had been planned (collaboratively) ahead of time. At other times, interactions were a dance, with adults and children responding to what they saw, offering assistance and making suggestions without being asked. There were no rules other than responding in ways that demonstrated understanding and caring.

Classroom practices at Betsy Miller developed from teachers' commitment to putting children at the center of their work. This shared commitment was supported by the Prospect Center for Education and Research and nurtured by Pat Carini's frequent consultations at the school. Carini's description of teaching as "deep play . . . loved work" (2001, p. 110) was reflected in how teachers talked about what they did. Caring provided the foundation for the narrative assessment process and other classroom practices and schoolwide structures that emerged from their work with Prospect. This led to an understanding of how tracking, labeling, and segregation interferes with caring by pathologizing children and denying "the humanness of error and the humanness of strong desire" (Carini, 2001, p. 69).

Unconditional caring did, however, not translate into permissiveness. Rather, caring for children at Betsy Miller reflected what Ruddick (1980/1999) describes as "maternal practice" (p. 370). This calls on adults to be attentive and responsive to sometimes conflicting and ever-changing demands. These include the need to provide guidance to assure children's safety and acceptability in the community. Allowing children to explore *only* their own interests and behave however they choose does not promote growth. At the same time, too much protection and direction will limit development. Understanding this dilemma, caregivers need to know children intimately and assess the contexts of their lives in and out of school to determine the kinds of experience to provide in their classrooms. To do this, Betsy Miller's teachers applied what Ruddick calls "attentive love" (p. 375), developing classroom practices that integrated information from colleagues and parents with their own experience of individual children.

The qualities that characterized teachers' relationships with children were mirrored in the kinds of relationships they established with one another. It wasn't just children who worked with one another on projects and other collaborative activities, but rather there was continual verbal and nonverbal interaction between and among children and adults. These interactions paid close attention to "caring for" the other (Noddings, 1984). Individual differences were considered and accommodated. This was as true in the way teachers shared responsibilities with one another as in how they interacted with children. The coexistence of collaboration and autonomy allowed adults to work in ways that best suited their needs, while maintaining collaborative relationships. This was also evident in multiple and overlapping collaborations between children and in the kind of individualization that provided ongoing support for every student. Balancing collaboration with individual needs and skills created a dialectical relationship that was central to how the school operated. Adults and children were living and working together, maintaining a dynamic tension between collectivism and individualism.

A shared history also deepened relationships and strengthened the school's culture. This didn't mean relationships were always positive. At times, conflicts emerged between teachers, collaborators, and paraprofessionals that couldn't be resolved. Compromise was often required, and on occasion the inability of individuals to work together led to shifting teams, changing collaborators, or leaving the school. The story that follows recounts this history. It is not presented as a formula for others but rather demonstrates the central role of collaboration, collegiality, and caring in creating and sustaining an inclusive school.

CHAPTER 3

Years of Chaos

The perspectives of teachers and administrators presented in this chapter reveal the relationship between the school's history and teachers' commitments to collaboration, collegiality, and compassionate caring. Beginning as a response to externally imposed reforms, the processes embedded in their stories would become as much a part of the school's culture as specific classroom practices and schoolwide structures. Deal and Peterson (1999) describe similar processes in their research on the development of school cultures:

> Cultural patterns and traditions evolve over time. They are initiated as the school is founded and thereafter shaped by critical incidents, forged through controversy and conflict and crystallized through triumph and tragedy. Culture takes form as, over time, people cope with problems, stumble onto rituals and routines, and create traditions and ceremonies to underlying values and beliefs. (p. 48)

PERSPECTIVES ON THE EVOLUTION
OF A CULTURE OF INCLUSION

The personal reflections of teachers and administrators presented in the following pages provide insights into the meaning of events that shaped Betsy Miller and reveal a web of interconnections that deepens our understanding of its culture (Geertz, 1973). Because they speak in voices other teachers can understand, I have chosen to present verbatim accounts of teachers' experiences. As is often the case in research offering teacher narratives (Berres et al., 1996; Connelly & Clandinin, 1988; Dorsch, 1998; Lieberman, 1995; Miller; 1990; Witherell & Noddings, 1991), the intentions of those whose voices are presented were not to provide specific directions to others struggling with similar issues. The teachers I spoke with neither positioned themselves as experts nor believed they had definitive answers to what they understood as complex and intractable problems. Rather, they saw themselves and their school as "in process" and believed that teachers at other schools interested in becoming more inclusive needed to pave their own paths. Their intentions were neither to liberate nor empower anyone else.

The individuals interviewed were consistently identified by other teachers, administrators, and parents as instrumental to transforming the school. They were also acknowledged as active participants or leaders in documents describing pivotal events, workshops, and grants during the years most central to the school's transformation (1987–1995). When interviewed, 6 of the 10 teachers were lead teachers: All 6 were female; 5 were White, and 1 was African American. Another African American woman was serving as acting principal at Betsy Miller when interviewed (1994–1995) but had been a classroom teacher there for the preceding 7 years. Collectively, they represented each grade level (K–5) and every instructional team. (One of the 5 White teachers had been a special education teacher at Betsy Miller during an earlier period.) The 3 other teachers interviewed included a male White teacher of English as a second language, a female White special education support teacher, and a female African American assistant teacher who had served as administrative assistant to Joe Stefano from 1987 through 1994. Their years of teaching experience ranged from 12 to 30 years. All but 2 had been at Betsy Miller for at least 10 years. Two of the African American women first came to the school in 1987 with Joe Stefano, when he became its principal. One left in 1992 and the other in 1994; both returned in 2002. Joe Stefano was interviewed several times. Marion Rusk, a European American woman who was principal at Betsy Miller from 1983 through 1984, was also interviewed.

The interview process provided an opportunity for these individuals to explore experiences, deepen commitments, and develop new insights into the development of the school. The process we engaged in was frequently recursive, jumping from one event to another, spanning years and connecting earlier experiences to current events. At times interviews became collaborative conversations, characterized by the kind of give-and-take discursive style teachers at Betsy Miller generally used with one another. Their willingness to engage in this kind of familiar conversational style reflected the rapport we had established during the time I spent at the school. The analysis that follows evolved from a compilation of these interactive narratives triangulated with field notes from observations in the school and surrounding community, documents from local newspapers, archival materials related to the school's history, and less formal discussions with these and other members of the Betsy Miller community.

Although the collective data tell a consistent story, I recognize it as incomplete. Missing are the voices of many other teachers, parents, students, administrators, and paraprofessionals. Although the perspectives of three African American women are included, it is important to keep in mind, given the significance of race in this school's development, that the majority of those interviewed were White teachers and administrators. Recognizing the impossibility of speaking to everyone and representing all voices equally, I attempted to limit distortion by triangulating the transcription data from formal interviews with information obtained in more informal conversations with other teachers at the school, past and present school district administrators, parents, and other community members. These included other African American men and women. Archival materials and local newspaper accounts of events impacting on the school and school district were also used to maximize the trustworthiness of what I had been told and the credibility of my interpretations (Lincoln & Guba, 1985). In spite of this, what follows still represents only partial truth (Marcus & Fischer, 1986). I believe, however, it is a story that needs telling. Even half-told stories are important when they reveal the realities of those who, like many teachers, may not yet have a public voice (Wolf, 1992).

In the midst of the research, the sudden death of Joe Stefano confirmed what teachers know about school life, but which I had failed to consider in my rationally conceived research plan: schools don't operate as linear, rationally conceived organizations or follow predictable paths. Rather, they are places where children and adults live out their lives in interaction with one another, in unpredictable ways. They are continually changing. Once I began writing, I would freeze time, making it impossible to capture the recursive nature of the school's development. I knew that while I was doing fieldwork and after I stopped, the school would continue to evolve. New families, children, and staff would enter and leave, changing the reality I was attempting to understand. The world surrounding the school would also change and continue to require renegotiation by teachers, parents, and children. The school would still be "in process." And yet, to tell the story of the school and its teachers, I needed to begin and end somewhere.

And so I begin by describing the context that provided the impetus for creating an inclusive culture. The story of its development does not recount a rationally conceived plan for reform and restructuring. Rather, it reflects a process that continued evolving as I studied its evolution. The dilemma I faced in trying to capture the story of a school in flux was in fact similar to the struggle teachers confronted daily: attempting to maintain a culture in a climate of constant change. This required a commitment to the values and beliefs that supported practice, in spite of imposed reforms. Responding to external demands would become as much a part of the school's culture as classroom practices and schoolwide structures.

THE LANDSCAPE

It's not unusual in this university town to identify a neighborhood by the elementary school whose attendance area it represents. Real estate agents are so aware of the importance of neighborhood schools that in August 2002 they sponsored an advertising supplement to the local newspaper, reporting every school's performance on statewide standardized tests alongside half-page ads for houses. Realtors knew that the university and college that employ the majority of the town's 30,000 permanent residents and bring an additional 25,000 students to the area each year provide a clientele for whom education is a central concern. The intellectual and political climate of the community also brings a highly charged atmosphere to all public issues. Decisions regarding everything from the profound to the ridiculous are fodder for public debate. Should "big-box" development be supported in the outskirts of town? Should the old bricks that lined downtown streets be replaced with asphalt? Should women be allowed to be topless in city parks? Every concern sparks intense public discussion. None, however, become as polarizing as those regarding public education. Strong rhetoric reflects divisions among academics, intellectuals, political activists, and artists, whose ideologies represent very different social and political perspectives toward education. Regardless of their differences, these people represent constituencies of privilege and power. They understand the ways schools work and how school systems operate, and are able to rally support for their points of view. They exert considerable political pressure on the school district's central office.

Their political prowess stands in sharp contrast to the position of families (with children under age 18) living in poverty that represent 19.5% of the town's population. Included among both the affluent and poor are nonnative speakers of English and non-Whites. Of the total population, 74% is White, 13.7% Asian, 6.7% African American, 5.3% Hispanic, and 0.04% Native American (U.S. Bureau of the Census, 2000). Adults from low-income families work in minimum-wage service sector jobs or receive public assistance. They care deeply about their children's education, but have less access to power than more affluent and better educated parents. They do, however, have activist allies among progressive parents and teachers with whom they have, at times, joined forces. The history of Betsy Miller reflects the ways in which some of these alliances have and have not succeeded in shaping its culture.

The two buildings that make up the Betsy Miller School sit on a grassy hillside in the midst of the middle-class, professional community known as the "Betsy Miller neighborhood." Visitors to the three-story, vintage-1926, redbrick schoolhouse that is its main building are greeted by a painting of a little red schoolhouse on the wall next to its front entrance and a bill-board on the front lawn that states simply, "Welcome to Betsy Miller." Its hand-painted letters are surrounded by primary-colored childlike drawings of a racially diverse group of children. This public celebration of the diversity found among the children inside the building is similarly highlighted on the large mural painted by students, teachers, and parents on the brick wall at the back of the school. That mural faces a wooden playground complex designed and constructed by parent and community volunteers.

Although the center of the mural represents an idyllic countryside with green hills, trees, lakes, and waterfalls, its message is explicitly political. Within the painting, multiethnic and multiracial groups of children and adults play, read, or look blissfully into the horizon. Possible sources of pollution are, however, evident in the landscape along the streams and forests that surround them. A large city skyline representing the cities many families of children at the school left behind is placed in the upper right-hand corner. The frame surrounding the painting is composed of small squares that depict women and men whose lives have been dedicated to promoting social justice (Mother Teresa, Aung San Suu Kyi, Harriet Tub-man, Wilma Mankiller, Gandhi, Nelson Mandela, Martin Luther King), ethnic and multicultural designs and symbols, a Palestinian and Israeli flag touching each other, and a multiracial group of children shaking hands with soldiers wearing different uniforms. Joe Stefano's portrait is painted in the central square at the top of the frame.

SHIFTS AND RIFTS

These public displays of community involvement and support for diversity and social justice are relatively recent additions. The two buildings that make up the Betsy Miller School may look the same as when they were built in 1926 and 1969, but what went on inside during my visits only began to take shape in 1983. The school district's redistricting plan, announced that year, would mark the end of a school that served only children from the surrounding middle-class and professional neighborhood. Betsy Miller would merge with the Harold Dodge Elementary School. One hundred children of international graduate students living in the nearby university housing project, many of whom did not speak English, would also be transferred here.

Harold Dodge stood in sharp contrast to Betsy Miller. Its neighbor-hood was home to low-income and working-class families, including the majority of the African Americans who live in this small city. In 1983 approximately 70% of the students attending Harold Dodge were African

American. Its student body was drawn from the neighborhood surrounding the school and included children from families where English was not the dominant language—recent refugees and others who had relocated from larger urban areas. In 1969 Harold Dodge adopted what it called an *open-school* philosophy, removing walls between some of its classrooms. That same year, the annex at Betsy Miller had also been constructed with an open-space design. Its commitment to openness was, however, somewhat different. The concept of child-centeredness expressed at Betsy Miller was accompanied by the expectation that students came to school prepared with basic academic skills and appropriate behavior. This expectation was largely fulfilled by a population of students who understood and internalized the "culture of power" reflected in public schools (Delpit, 1988). Student discipline and basic academic skills were not concerns of its teachers and parents.

In contrast, the kind of open education found at Harold Dodge was described by its principal, Marion Rusk, as having "flexibility of time and space but not of subject matter." In response to parental concerns, the school gradually moved from student-centered instructional approaches to teaching academic skills in a traditional, teacher-directed manner. Parents from the community had become very involved in the school's development and wanted to be assured that their children were developing basic academic skills. As their principal, Marion Rusk responded to these concerns. The following is taken from her personal journal, in which she documented her experiences at Harold Dodge and described the nature of the commitment she shared with families:

> A commitment that we [at Harold Dodge] have with the community that probably is number one is for basic education for children. The community expects the children will get the fundamentals of reading, writing, and arithmetic. When our parents were asked about traditional schools in a questionnaire, many responded, "My child goes to a traditional school. It's Harold Dodge." The parents are very involved in working on the educational program with us, especially Title I, and each year at about this time [spring] we review where we've been, what we're doing, and begin to make changes.
>
> Another shared commitment is caring for the young child—the total child. The breakfast program, the lunch program, the after-school program have been developed by a parent co-op. The total child—the child being totally looked at—is a shared commitment.
>
> The building itself over the years has been especially important to parents. Its location: it stands for security; always there and always

open. I think another commitment is the power, the autonomy that parents sense has been developed over these past years.

The decision to close Harold Dodge and three other small elementary schools was, in part, motivated by the school district's concerns for efficiency during a time of economic decline. A reduced school-age population had left each of its 12 elementary schools with fewer children than they were originally designed to serve. Heating and lighting buildings during the cold, dark winter months was seen as too costly to justify keeping class sizes small (fewer than 20 in each class). The choice of which schools to close was, however, very politicized. Closing Harold Dodge was also one way the city could respond to being cited for maintaining a racially segregated school system. As elsewhere in the United States, segregation in the schools reflected the racially segregated nature of surrounding neighborhoods.

While many progressive and liberal-minded individuals saw closing Dodge as a positive move toward racial desegregation, the responses of parents from the African American community were quite different. The recollections of Marion Rusk, informal discussions with people involved with the 1983 school closings, and archival materials (newspaper accounts, minutes and reports from school board and community meetings) reveal parental dismay and anger. In her interview, Rusk described the merger plan as inciting "a pitched battle in every neighborhood." Although there were public hearings, she believed that the school board had already made up its mind to close her school and that public meetings only served to "divide and conquer." Many in the Dodge community believed that the school district's decisions were not promoted by concerns for equity but rather were influenced by the resale value of buildings. Other older school buildings had previously been renovated and turned into apartments, office buildings, and shopping centers. Harold Dodge was in a prime location for commercial development. Clearly some communities had more influence than others in the final decision about which schools were to be closed.

Although it would have been considered politically incorrect for liberal and progressive parents at Betsy Miller to openly oppose busing low-income, minority, and non-English-speaking children to their school, informal conversations with neighborhood residents and written commentaries from that time document publicly articulated concerns about overcrowding. Some parents did not want to change the nature of their school to accommodate its newest students. There had been some discussion about moving the prekindergarten classrooms from Dodge into the early childhood annex, and moving the kindergarten through second grades from the

Annex into the main building. Parents' objections to the loss of library space and conversions of art and music rooms into classrooms kept the existing early childhood focus of the Annex intact. Dodge's prekindergarten program was put at another school.

Although the following statement, taken from a note written by a parent in 1984 to Marion Rusk after she became the principal of Betsy Miller, is the only written evidence I found indicating concern with the academic competence of the newer students, conversations with local parents and teachers revealed that other parents shared these concerns:

> There will hopefully be no sacrifice to the gifted children who are *way* above grade level, at the expense of acculturating the new group—I mean not to be so concerned with merger activities, folk art, and so on at the expense of computers, literature groups, and advanced math. I am very concerned about the heavy arts influence from the other school, because the school district does not have g & t [gifted and talented] well enough established in the core subjects.

THE HUMAN SIDE OF CHANGE

During the 1982–83 school year, students from Harold Dodge visited Betsy Miller several times, attended joint assembly programs, and participated in community arts projects. Marion Rusk angrily described these activities as "surface attempts" to prepare students, parents, and teachers for the merger. She punned cynically, "They were just shows. Sitting together in assemblies did not deal with breaking down barriers and promoting diversity." There were also attempts to bring parents together and develop a combined Parent Teacher Association (PTA). Both schools had PTAs and active parent involvement. Creating an active PTA at Dodge had, however, required years of building trust and creating a school where neighborhood parents felt safe and respected. On the other hand, no one had to encourage Betsy Miller's parents to form a PTA. They were familiar with and comfortable in academic settings and placed many demands on teachers and administrators. They wanted more enrichment, arts programs, and advanced academics. Student discipline and basic skills were not their central concern. Rusk believed that these very different perspectives created disputes that led parents from Henry Dodge to believe they were "not expected to be an active part of the merger." Despite efforts by school personnel, there was "very little interaction between parents." Combined meetings with teachers from both schools were held in the year preceding the merger, presenting options to teachers. Although most teachers from

Dodge would move to Betsy Miller with Rusk when she became its principal, they felt like outsiders. Records from combined staff meetings do not
indicate any in-depth discussions regarding curriculum or collaborative efforts toward significant restructuring of existing programs. Rather, the emphasis was letting teachers from Dodge know how things were done at
Betsy Miller. The multiage classrooms, teacher-directed approaches to instruction, parent participation, emphasis on diversity and arts' programs
central to Harold Dodge were not discussed. Weekly staff meetings, parent
conferencing, and teaming that supported the mainstreaming of children
identified for special education at Dodge would not be continued at Betsy
Miller.

Attempts to prepare students, teachers, and parents for the merger
were conceived by school district officials as a means to bring key stakeholders together to establish a shared community. Key players from both
communities were not, however, involved in planning any of these activities. The differences between the communities that each school represented
and the psychological meaning of the merger were not acknowledged. District officials failed to consider the deeply personal identification and attachment each constituency had to its respective school. The culture of one
school was clearly favored over the other. This favoritism reflected power
dynamics and institutional racism familiar to parents and teachers from
Dodge. The needs and interests of the children of affluent, well-educated,
White, English-speaking adults would once again take precedence over
those of their children.

Evans's (1996) analysis of the "human side of school change" provides
insights into the difficulties teachers, parents, and students from both
schools faced during the first years of the merger. He points out how rationally conceived plans for school restructuring, such as those that led to
combining these two schools, generally ignore the emotional significance
of change. Events and experiences that are part of people's lives for long
periods of time take on great emotional significance. Neighborhood
schools are often associated with these kinds of experiences by teachers
who have been there for many years, as well as by parents whose children
attend these schools. Change threatens the "structures of meaning" (p. 30)
these individuals create to give meaning to their experiences. These deep
structures become integrated into their personal understandings of reality
and shape the way they think and feel about the world.

Not acknowledging or addressing the perceived threats to security experienced during periods of significant change does not make them disap-
pear. Instead, denial contributes to experiencing change as loss and can
intensify resistance. The communities that these schools represented had
become inseparable from the ways staff defined their roles. Their personal

belief systems were embedded at the primary level of both schools' cultures, sustaining and reinforcing one another. Work experiences had become inseparable from personal experiences. The personal meaning staff attributed to their jobs reflected how they defined themselves, shaped their roles, and maintained relationships with one another, parents, and children.

It should not be surprising, then, that many of the teachers from both schools experienced the 1983 merger as a loss. The importance of their relationships with one another had been neither considered in the decision to combine these two schools nor addressed in the orientation programs. Parents from each school were wary of those from the other. Their distrust reflected the racism and classism intricately woven into the fabric of American life and reflected in its schools. It should also not be surprising—given the lack of enthusiasm among the staff at each school, the differences between the ways their schools operated, and the disparities between the communities they represented—that the first years of the merger were catastrophic.

Suzanne Millman, a European American, had been a kindergarten teacher at Harold Dodge for 3 years before it was closed. When the schools combined, she transferred to Betsy Miller and would remain there for 18 years, until her retirement in 2002. In the following statement, she offers her recollection of what happened during the first years of the merger. Other teachers, administrators, and parents involved with either school during those years, supported her comments. In the following statement, she describes the impact of the differences between the ways teachers responded to the communities represented by their schools.

> The principal who had been [at Betsy Miller] left. Marion Rusk came up from Dodge so we had a new principal. You had six or seven new teachers coming in, you had a new school population coming in that was very different from the population that had been here. There was a lot of resentment, because as it turned out the people who had lost their school were the people who had used Harold Dodge as a neighborhood community center. They felt very strongly that their school worked down there. Parents had access to it, they could walk to it, but the folks up on the hill had the political clout and they won. That's how it falls out, but you can't necessarily be too pleased about it. And I wouldn't say that teachers were mad at teachers about that because they were fairly realistic. We all know who's gonna win this battle. We're gonna fight to do the right thing but we all know who's gonna end up winning. There was no rancor over that. It was just a political reality that everybody was disgusted with but we knew it was gonna happen that way.

Although she didn't see overt rancor between the teachers, Suzanne recognized how differences in the communities they served were reflected in the way they perceived their roles. The failure to address these differences would soon lead to conflicts and a high turnover among teachers.

Suzanne: These were very different populations, and the teachers who had been teaching [the Betsy Miller] population didn't have the skills to work with the downtown kids. The teachers from downtown had skills that were very applicable for low-income children but didn't go over too big with the kids who were used to having it a lot looser, having a lot more input.

Judy: So would you describe Betsy Miller as being sort of a progressive, open kind of a school during that time?

Suzanne: Yes, that's what they tried to do, but I don't think they did it very well. Because of the school population and who you were drawing from, a lot more latitude could be in operation. The kids were very socialized to following a middle-class agenda.

Judy: So, are you saying you would describe it as a traditional curriculum in the sense of using workbooks and textbooks?

Suzanne: Yes, a traditional curriculum, but sort of an open kind of an attitude. Whereas the Dodge group [of teachers] had a real strong background in direct instruction, and didn't do a lot of touchy-feely stuff. Their teaching style was so different. Basically, however you want to look at that sort of stuff, the folks at Dodge had a lot more parent comfort. There was a parent comfort level.

Judy: Were there more African American teachers at Dodge?

Suzanne: Only one that I can remember off the top of my head. It wasn't that the teachers were Black, it was their [neighborhood] school, and the doors were open. And [parents] made sure it worked like that.

There was a lot a philosophical clash between teaching methods or styles of teaching, even though both were pretty traditional. So there was conflict over teaching styles, and Dodge teachers going more for direct instruction, phonics, whatever. Get that stuff out. And the nice middle-class kids whose moms and dads read to them every night and took them to the city, you know, just didn't care for it much. And of course, nothing quite worked, and we would lose a teacher a year. I was the union rep. at the time for this building. And it's really hard when you lose a teacher.

Judy: How would you lose them? Would they transfer out or would they retire, or get fired, or be asked to leave, or ... ?

Suzanne: The first one that I remember really clearly was a person who could not handle the children and didn't see any other way of looking at the class than the way she knew. So she resorted to taking children by the hand or something. She had been upset for a while, but she took a child by the hand and the child twisted out of her hand in such a way that she felt like her hand was hurt, and she was very upset.

Well, the child was Black and she was White, and she was so upset she wanted to put something in writing. So I let her put it in writing, with a pretty clear idea of how this was going to unfold itself. The teacher's hand was hurt. She was very upset.

Judy: What grade was this?

Suzanne: Kindergarten.

Judy: Well, this woman, this kindergarten teacher, did she get transferred to another school?

Suzanne: No, she quit, she didn't come back. That was losing a teacher; it's unpleasant, even when you want that teacher to get lost; it's not fun.

Other teachers would retire or ask for transfers to other schools. Losing teachers had a negative impact on the morale of teachers who had been at Betsy Miller long before the merger, reinforcing the feeling that they were losing their school. The relationships they had with one another were threatened.

OUT OF SIGHT, OUT OF MIND

Rachel Meyer, a European American, was the special education support teacher at Betsy Miller before the merger and remained there until her retirement in 1995. Her job included coordinating programs and services for children classified for special education and remedial services. Before 1983, the relatively small number of children with special needs and the nature of their needs had made her job manageable. This all changed after the merger.

What happened was we had a curriculum that was a White, middle-class curriculum. We had not a sense at all about what to do with suddenly over 100 ESL kids, more than 90 Title I children. We had at least 60 kids who were special ed. We really were very well intentioned. We wanted to meet the needs of all the children, so we had all these specialists running around, and we had a resource room for special ed, and a Title I teacher for Title I kids, and an ESL room for ESL kids. . . . The worst-case scenario was a kid who went to all of these services including O.T. and P.T., and speech and language; and the kids were never part of the mainstream curriculum. They never were part of the classroom community, and they were really outside of any loop, if there was a loop.

Rachel recognized that the values and beliefs underlying the classroom practices and schoolwide structures at Betsy Miller had neither included a commitment to serving all children in the general education program nor addressed the challenges many of the children from Harold Dodge presented. As Rachel stated,

> There was never anything that was really bad. It was really just acting up in class, being very sassy, talking back to teachers, running around, never being in their seats. Some of it was the whole environment in the classroom was really not very conducive to kids who had a lot of energy, and couldn't really connect with what was happening. So they used that energy to be restless and noncompliant, and mouthy.

The implications of race and social class to academic performance and classroom behavior had not been previously considered by most of Betsy Miller's teachers. To be effective with their new population of students, the staff needed to become interested and prepared for working with diverse and challenging groups of children. Teachers who weren't interested left and were replaced by new teachers like Wendall Warren, a European American. Assigned to Betsy Miller as a half-time teacher of English as a Second Language in 1984, Wendall would remain there until 2001. He became central to restructuring the way services were provided to children who were nonnative speakers of English. The conditions he found in 1984 reflected what he perceived as teacher's lack of preparation, knowledge, and concern for the large number of nonnative speakers of English who were transferred to the school. According to Wendall,

> I'd be at the other school in the mornings, and Betsy Miller in the afternoons. The program was pull-out. A lot of frustrations around scheduling, and around what I was beginning to perceive as lack of knowledge or awareness. For some people, the kids were just like guests, and they didn't have to invest in them at all. For some folks, it was, "They learn English and then I can work with them." For some, it was, "It's okay to have kids sitting in the back of the room doing tons of busy work because they can't do [the work I am giving the other kids]." Some teachers expected me to give them busy work

for the whole morning when I wasn't here, to keep the kids occupied.

There was a snow day, or some reason that I was over here in the morning, and I was walking down the hallway, and I saw three kids from this one classroom that I worked with, sitting out in the hallway doing these stacks of paper. I came over and I started talking to them because I thought they were in trouble. I just thought it was odd that they were sitting in the hallway working, so I talked to them, and the best I could find out was that's where they worked every day in the morning. They spent the morning in the hallway, working on these tons of paperwork. I immediately went . . . I was so livid I couldn't go to the teacher. I went to the principal, and I couldn't even explain. I just said, "Come with me." And we walked down the hallway, and I said, "What do you see here?" And she said, "Well, I see kids working there." And I said, "But look who's working there. They're all ESL kids. They've been singled out because they're not participating in whatever's going on in the classroom, and they shouldn't be here. They should be in the room."

So my feeling in terms of the school here at that time, it was out of sight, out of mind, there were a lot of hidden messages in where the kids worked, things around being visible or not visible, things around what my role was as a teacher, but especially the kids and what the expectations were for the kids.

There was a good deal of misunderstanding among staff about the lives of some students Wendall worked with. Their families' association with the university led many teachers to believe that most of these children came from privileged circumstances. This stereotyping led to overlooking the difficult personal situations many children faced and misunderstanding the sociocultural dimensions of their learning experiences. Wendall elaborated on the background of his students:

It changes from year to year, but generally when I've paid close attention, generally about 80–85% had a university connection, and the other 15–20% were refugees, immigrants, or folks born in the United States who have a heritage language at home.

But the stereotype here was not of the struggling immigrant refugee family. The stereotype was ESL synonymous with the university, and that was synonymous with privilege. Even within that, there were many, many instances where that didn't play out, where the family was here but they were economically deprived while they were here. Or, they come and university housing only allows two children, and they have to decide which of their kids to leave behind. Families that are used to an extended arrangement for taking care of their kids suddenly are thrown into a nuclear family setting. So there's that stereotype of having everything going well for you, but there were a lot of families, and still are, that can be under all kinds of stresses that are below the surface. The surface is, you must be privileged to have made it here, and therefore you must be privileged while you are here. Also in terms of kids' family life at home, once a parent is thrown into a student role, in terms of time, a lot may not be able to devote much to kids in terms of time. Some families handle that well, and some don't.

Materially the environments can be comparable to an impoverished environment, where you go in and it's a bare room, a mattress or something. Again, that's exceptional, but certainly within the university piece of that population there were things like that going on.

Wendall also found that although some teachers welcomed new ideas for working with students who had limited English language proficiency, others were quite resistant to his suggestions. He was not initially aware of the ways his presence represented a threat.

Back in 1984, I was new. This was my first time doing ESL in elementary, and I really didn't know what I was doing. I had instincts, but I was being pulled in a lot of different directions. There was a program very much in use here at the time, which was the antithesis of setting up conditions for language learning; but because it had been sold that way, [the idea] that this—the DISTAR program—was good for language learning was entrenched. And what it was, was taking language and decontextualizing it and making into as small bits as possible. It had all this so-called scientific research to support it, and then additionally the kicker was that a lot of it had been developed in use with Spanish-speaking children of the 1960s. And it was very behaviorist, and working with small pieces, it was very limiting. That was so entrenched here, in both schools [where I was assigned], but especially here.

In our ESL meetings we would rail against this program, and our coordinator at the time clearly saw the discrepancy in this really working. Well, I had a parent conference one day and I was late getting to a staff meeting, and she had come to a [full] staff meeting, and she had presented all the rationale for reasons why this program should be discarded, but she hadn't done any of the political footwork that you need to do. So she basically came in and attacked a core piece of the school's identity—the staff. It was just across the board in the school, but she came at it from why this was not appropriate for ESL kids. But the implication is that it wasn't for anyone and it became connected with the general sense of disorder.

The threat many Betsy Miller teachers associated with Harold Dodge students, teachers, and parents, and the stereotypes held of children who were non-English speakers continued to interfere with the creation of a cohesive learning environment. It would take several years before teachers could begin to work with one another to resolve the tension and conflict that characterized the school during the first years after the merger, and create a new culture. A commitment to working with one another and a willingness to embrace change was required.

THE LEADERSHIP VOID

Appointed as Betsy Miller's principal in 1983, Marion Rusk found herself unable to bring the two schools together. She left in frustration during her second year. In the minds of those teachers who had been at Betsy Miller before the merger, she represented Harold Dodge and its community. A principal who was not identified with either school was needed. Bringing in outsiders from within the district's pool of administrators would, however, prove equally ineffective. None of the three principals brought in during the next 2 years had the kinds of skills this job demanded. Suzanne, the kindergarten teacher quoted above, describes how ineffective leadership heightened the problems facing teachers:

> The first and second year, it was still Marion. Then came Tom
> O'Hara. I think we lost a teacher that year. . . . Teachers that were
> close to retirement were beginning to retire. So the next year—it was
> that spring—he left, and we had the principal who got hospitalized
> with tubes in both arms, and then we got a replacement principal.
> And we had an awful school psychologist who was just the pits, the
> absolute pits. I can't even remember his name we hated him so much.
> And then the crossing guard was arrested for child molestation. So,
> they're looking for another principal to *shove* [emphasis mine] into
> the school, and they send another guy whose wife was really sick. He
> looks at us and says, "I don't want to be here, and I'm sure you can
> understand I don't need any more stress in my life." And then we are
> saying, "Well, nobody loves us, right?"

Teachers saw themselves being manipulated by the school district's central office and stopped expecting any meaningful assistance and support. Those who didn't transfer to other schools or retire accepted the challenges presented by their students and the sometimes-strained relationships between one another as their daily reality. They didn't like what was happening at the school but felt powerless to change much beyond their own classrooms. To survive, they relied on the age-old default position taken by teachers: stay in your room, close your door, and do what you believe is best. They had experienced too many ineffective administrators and supervisors blaming them for students' problems. By the third year after the merger they had received the message that the problems at the school were evidence of their inability to teach and control students. In the following remarks, Suzanne identifies what she began to see as the gendered nature of the conflicts with superiors; sexism and powerlessness had become intertwined:

> [The psychologist] was a womanizer; he was sexist. His answer for
> any kind of academic problem was to put the kid on DISTAR. He
> slapped [a teacher] in the face one day for arguing with him. He and
> one of the principals brought champagne into the school one day
> when we had a before-school meeting, and we all thought it was
> highly inappropriate. Even after school we would have thought it was
> a little questionable, but before school? I'm sorry, that's just not ac-
> ceptable, that's weird. And he would touch people. He would touch
> women. He didn't do it to me, because I was his age, but he did it to
> the younger women. And you could see them just cringing, but they
> didn't know how to tell him to stop. So we hated him. He would
> walk into the staff room and head for one of the younger teachers,
> and we would just . . . the older teachers should have said something.
> But anyway, so we hated him, to the point where I can't remember
> his name.

In the following statement, Sandy Walden, a teacher who came to Betsy Miller from Harold Dodge in 1983 and was still teaching there in 2002, describes the lack of safety she felt as a teacher during the 1986–87 academic year:

> We had four principals. The year before, one of them was a very
> lovely man who was losing his mind, couldn't remember the teachers'
> names; he was ill. Our custodian had been arrested for inappropri-
> ately touching children, there were fights in the halls. I used to walk
> into the [main] building and hide, because it was scary to be there.
> There was no respect of teachers, of children, of families; there was a
> complete breakdown.

Her reflections reveal a sense of powerlessness and fear reminiscent of many women's reluctance to walk home alone at night on a dark street. Clearly, something needed to change. Before teachers could teach and students could learn, they needed to feel safe. Everyone agreed that something needed to be done to turn the school around; it was in chaos.

FILLING THE LEADERSHIP VOID

The school district responded to the problems at Betsy Miller in the fashion typical of hierarchical school bureaucracies: they hired another principal. Joe Stefano was picked for the job in 1987. He would be the fifth principal since the merger 4 years earlier. He transferred there, somewhat reluctantly, from another elementary school with a large population of low-income, rural children. His previous success at restructuring two other elementary schools with low-income populations and his public commitment to educational equity made him a logical candidate. Ironically, what he had learned from his other successes was that he could not turn around a failing school on his own. He needed teachers who shared his vision, were willing to take risks, and were able to create a new school culture.

Quakie Onaygo was one of the African American teachers Joe brought with him to Betsy Miller in 1987. In the following narrative, she recounts her history with Joe, the events that led to their coming to Betsy Miller, and what she found once she got there. Her story demonstrates the way in which Joe's relationships with teachers became central to what they were eventually able to accomplish together:

> The first person to hire me as a professional was Joe Stefano. That was in 1978. Then the Hillside Elementary School still existed. I was doing my student teaching in that building. I was obviously a nontraditional student. I was married with a child. My senior project involved organizing the entire school in a multicultural play, or production, as it turned out to be. And Joe hadn't really heard the term multicultural before, but he apparently liked what he saw. I was still student teaching and he offered me a job on the spot. And I said, "When?" and he said, "Now." I said, "But I'm still a student," and he said, "We can work around that." Apparently a teacher had to go on a medical leave and he wanted me to take over. So that was our first journey together. That goes back about 3 decades—let's see, how old is my daughter? That's 25 years ago. That was our first experience together.
>
> The following year they closed the sixth-grade classrooms in the

elementary schools, and [I went to the middle school] for 9 years and probably would have stayed, but Joe came calling one day. . . . The administration at that time was targeting schools whose test scores were really low. And they knew they needed a very progressive, real innovative principal to kind of helm the ship. So, of course, they singled out Joe and he was given great latitude about hiring. I was a nondriver at the time. He decided that I needed to be the person to head up his intermediate team, and the school was [a small rural elementary school]. I said, "Joe, there is no way I'm going there. I don't do country, I don't do the cows, and I don't drive." So he says, "I'll teach you to drive. You'll get used to the country, and you'll ignore the cows." And so we went on that venture together.

That was an extraordinary experience. In fact, it was one of my turnaround experiences in education. That was the school that helped me to understand that anyone can teach anyone's child if you believe in the child. Up until that time, I really felt that students of color, particularly students of African American descent, needed to be taught only by African American teachers. Everything I had seen up until that point, everything I had researched up until that point, was so clear to me that unskilled, culturally illiterate staff did more damage to students of color than good. And a lot of kids ended up in special ed. A lot of kids ended up on the Title I rolls—not because they weren't capable students but because they had teachers who did not tap into them from a cultural perspective. Great mistakes were made because of that.

So, being a townie, there were certain places I was trained not to go. I grew up in the 1950s and 1960s here, and [that country school was in] one of the places that African Americans did not go. We were well aware that Klan meetings took place there in my childhood. It wasn't a community that was open to people of color. I certainly was flooded with all the stereotypes of it being a redneck community, and they were either card-carrying John Birch Society members or Klan members. So I just couldn't see going into that environment. Also, it required taking my daughter, who was in second grade, with me. I was very reluctant to take her into an environment where she would hear lots of racial epithets thrown at her on a regular basis. But when Joe Stefano decides that he wants you to join his mission, there's no saying no. So he helped teach me how to drive, and I had to buy my first car and drive out there.

It was an extraordinary experience. And when I say it was a fork in the road, it was because those kids, who are well into their 30s now, still stay in touch with me. These were the little country kids that were the throwaway kids of the district on the other side of the coin. And their parents weren't valued and the kids weren't valued. I don't know what great strides I made in race relations, but certainly their parents understood that they had a teacher that cared enormously about their kids, invested in their kids. And that's what they reacted to.

So I was there for 2 years and Joe was handed a new mission. He had gotten the scores up, turned the school around, really stabilized it, and he said one day, "I'm going to get a sub and I need you to take a ride with me." So we came to Betsy Miller and there were kids running all over the building. I mean, I don't think I had ever walked into a school where there was more chaos than that first day I walked into that building. So I looked at Joe, and he says, "I think this is our next work."

"*Our* next work? Remember, I'm on loan from the middle school. I'm going back. I'm not doing this."

But he keeps saying, "Yep, this looks like our next mission. OK. We can do this."

"We, Joe? We? Joe, *we?*"

Needless to say, I ended up here. It was a school that had not only been leaderless, but they had actually merged two extremely different populations of kids. Of course the university bedroom kids were well orientated on how to behave in school. [Betsy Miller] had teachers who came from the class and certainly pedagogical background orientation that blended very well with that population of kids. [But then these students and teachers] merged with the Dodge population, which were the downtown kids who at that time were 70% African American and 30% White, who were kids from below the poverty line. There was no staff development around the merger. There was just no work done to bring these two very different faculties and these very different kids into this setting. And so it was just predictable that there would be nothing but pure chaos. My first observations in my first year with Joe was that the kids were truly in charge of the school . . . in a very unhealthy way.

And one of the ways that many of the teachers that I'd say were career Betsy Miller teachers dealt with that population of kids that just didn't fall into the program was to leave them in the hall. So they were out in the hall a great deal of the time. That was my first, strongest observation, that all the African American kids, particularly the males, were sitting in chairs out in the hall or running up and down the halls. Just completely out of control. It was an enormous task ahead of us—it really was. In a major way. . . .

So we were here from day one, and it was hard, *it was hard*. As a fifth-grade teacher, I was basically inheriting a population of kids who had already been socialized to see school as someplace not to take seriously and adults as people who could be manipulated; who had not experienced much success academically and totally disregarded any sense of the teacher as taking control and establishing the parameters of the environment. They were so used to establishing how things worked around here. In fact, the first day in school, there was a young man in my classroom who had been retained two times. So he was in fifth grade but he was 14 years old and he could practically pick up the desk on his knees when he sat down. And he said to me in front of everybody, "Ms. O. You have a family, right?"

"I do."

"You have kids, right?"

"I do."

"Don't put your effort into this. Put your effort into them. 'Cause this is not going to change."

"Is that the advice you have given all your teachers the first day?"

"No."

"So, why you givin' it to me?"

"Because the other ones knew. They let us outside to play all day."

"Let me tell you something. You will probably not see the outside until the last day of school."

And that's where it began. It was amazing at first. I started with the small, really turning around a population of kids that were just absolutely doomed in the public school system. And that was my only goal: to turn this population into viable learners. Get those test scores up; get them exited from Title I; get them declassified as emotionally disturbed; all that stuff so that they would at least have a fair shot when they went on to middle school. And especially having come from that environment, I knew too well what had to be under their belts. And Joe did too.

CHAPTER 4

From Chaos to
Collaborative Leadership

Those not directly involved in the daily life of Betsy Miller during the 7 years Joe Stefano was principal (1987–1994) present an image of a lone hero, coming into a school in disarray and single-handedly leading teachers out of chaos. Outsiders see him as someone who operated on his own, taking risks and challenging the status quo. Although no one disputes his importance as a catalyst for change nor the value of the support he provided, Joe's elevation to the status of hero in the general community conceals the true story of the school's development. It also fails to explain how teachers were able to sustain commitments to its inclusive culture once he left the school. As Biklen (1995) points out, portraying a school's leader as the "modernist hero" taking on an entrenched educational bureaucracy has served to reinforce gendered images of female teachers as passive followers of strong male leaders, and negates both the importance of teachers and the significance of collaboration, consensus building, and the development of school communities.

A more complete picture of Joe's role emerged as I spoke with him, talked to teachers, and examined documents describing what went on from the time he arrived in 1987 until his transfer in 1995. I discovered that he, in fact, provided the kind of leadership current researchers identify as essential for promoting change and supporting the development of inclusive schools (Kugelmass & Ainscow, 2003). Inclusion is increasingly seen as a key challenge for educational leaders. For example, Leithwood, Jantzi, and Steinbach (1999) suggest that with continuing diversity, schools need to thrive on uncertainty, have a greater capacity for collective problem solving, and be able to respond to a wider range of pupils. Fullan (2001) describes five mutually reinforcing components necessary for effective leadership in times of change: moral purpose, understanding the change process, relationship building, knowledge creation and sharing, and coherence making. Sergiovanni (1992) also points to the challenge of student diversity and argues that hierarchical and authoritarian approaches to school leadership may well be getting in the way of improvement efforts. He suggests that the tendency to view leadership as individual behavior rather than collective action and the emphasis on bureaucratic, psychological, and technical-rational authority for achieving change neglects the role of teachers' professional authority for creating lasting and positive change.

Adopting a similar perspective, Lambert et al. (2002) argue for a "constructivist" view of leadership. From their perspective, leadership involves an interactive process entered into by students and teachers as well as administrators. Consequently, there is a need for shared leadership, with the principal seen as a leader of leaders. Hierarchical structures are replaced by shared responsibility in a community that becomes characterized by agreed values and hopes. The control functions associated with school leadership become less important or even counterproductive.

Riehl (2000) develops "a comprehensive approach to school administration and diversity," focusing specifically on the work of school principals in inclusive settings. She concludes that school leaders need to attend to three broad types of tasks: fostering new meanings about diversity, promoting inclusive practices within schools, and building connections between schools and communities. Her analysis leads to a positive view of the potential for school principals to engage in inclusive, transformative developments. She states: "When wedded to a relentless commitment to equity, voice, and social justice, administrators' efforts in the tasks of sense making, promoting inclusive cultures and practices in schools, and building positive relationships outside of the school, may indeed foster a new form of practice" (p. 71).

Research by Spillane, Halverson, and Diamond (2001) expands upon these issues. Their work examines the complexity of school leadership and provides a theoretical framework for the kind of leadership that evolved at Betsy Miller. Their study of "distributed leadership" challenges the notion that school leadership resides in any one individual. They point out that although tasks may be performed by a single person, the impact of his or her actions on the organization reflects a variety of sociocultural features and demonstrates how "social context is an integral component, not just a container, for intelligent activity" (p. 23). Their research highlights the importance of looking beyond the school principal in understanding leadership practice in schools.

Although none of these researchers make explicit connections between their findings and feminist theory, each offers an understanding of leadership consistent with the structures, beliefs, and values underlying feminist organizational cultures (Halford & Leonard, 2001; Henry, 1996). Henry (1996) identifies features central to leadership in schools having a feminist orientation as focused on teaching and learning, emphasizing collaborative relationships, and building community among all stakeholders. In these schools, "all decision making, policy, and practice start from a notion of caring" (p. 182). Decision making is shared through dialogue and negotiation within a shared commitment to equity, justice, and fairness. Betsy Miller would become this kind of school.

COLLABORATIVE LEADERSHIP

Joe provided both the impetus for change and the support teachers needed to access resources and manage external pressures from local, state, and federal bureaucracies. He was not, however, solely responsible for changing the school, and he understood that without the right staff nothing would change. Suzanne Millman was the first to alert me to how I had internalized a heroic image of Joe in thinking he was solely responsible for changing the school. When asked to describe his role in transforming the school, she stopped me:

I'm thinking about how organizations are run and what we do in this country and maybe other countries as well. We see this as a structure, as a pyramidal structure, so that we see history occurring so that if you talk about important American history, you say of course we've got this Declaration of Independence, and who wrote that? Thomas Jefferson. Other important things that happen, like the civil rights movement: Martin Luther King. We perceive these as examples of the way change occurs in our history, and we perceive of history as being organized, the way all information is being organized. So we see all organizations work this way, all history works this way, all life works this way, and then it becomes a justification for a class system in our society, because this is the way it is.

In these messy collaborative efforts, [there is not any] one person without whom it never would have happened. . . . So I think we're so well programmed into thinking that this is the way change occurs, structures are organized. There is no 1 person you could identify, no 10 people you could identify, that if those 10 people had never been born, it still would have happened. In the U.S. Constitution, if 2 people had dropped dead on their way to the Convention, it still would have happened. Those instances of collaboration and joint effort, are not taught in our school, are not held up as the important way things are organized and happen. And it has social implications and class implications for opening up and being inclusive. This has implications for narrowing down and excluding. And we're so well trained—and I do mean that in the educational, trained way—so well trained as this being the only explanation of this, for the phenomena that occur. Even when it happens this way, we can't see it.—So, now I'll tell you about what *I* think happened at Miller.

BUILDING A CRITICAL MASS

Joe's first task would be establishing what he called a "critical mass" of teachers who were not only excellent educators but also concerned with issues of social justice, shared his belief that "schools were for children," and were willing to take risks. He understood that mistrust had been bred by previously imposed decisions and nurtured by experiences at the school since the merger. His first strategy was to temper teachers' skepticism by hiring teacher allies and other staff from his former school experiences. Among these was the European American school librarian, Marge Bowman, who would provide leadership in shifting approaches to literacy. She would redefine the role of school librarian to include helping teachers select children's literature and trade books for their classrooms. During the 1987–88 school year, each teacher would be given a budget of $1,000 to purchase books to replace basal readers and workbooks. By 1989, Marge would be assisting teachers in the use of "literature groups" with diverse groups of children.

Although rules and regulations regarding seniority and certification limited whom he could hire, Joe was masterful at manipulation in the interest of what he believed to be in the best interest of children. As Quakie pointed out, "He just intuitively knew that he needed to have a population of people in leadership roles that looked like the kids that were so underserved at that time." The following transcription from my interview with Elaine Cook ("Cookie"), an assistant teacher Joe brought to Betsy Miller during his first year, illustrates how he went about building a constituency of supporters. Elaine was an African American woman who had raised her children in the local community and worked with Joe as a teacher assistant at another elementary school. That school also had a significant population of African American children from low-income families and no teachers of color. Although she was neither a certified teacher nor administrator, he created a position at Betsy Miller that enabled her to provide culturally relevant support and caring for African American children and their families.

Elaine: Quakie was a teacher here, and she said, "Elaine, you got to help me man. It's crazy up here." Then Joe called me and said, "Cookie. You got to come and help me." So I left my other job in February, in the middle of the year. The kids were crazy here. There were little kids, African American children, that were running the school. If they had behavior problems, they were usually sent out of their classes. They had behavior problems, and they were sitting on the floors in the hallways. . . .

Well, Joe changed that policy. "I don't want to see kids in the hall, sitting on the floor, trying to get back in." It didn't help those kids at all. So he gave me the position of Administrative Assistant to the Principal. Now as Administrative Assistant to the Principal, I did most of the discipline.

Judy: Like a vice-principal?

Elaine: But I didn't have the credentials for it. So, I was just an assistant. Principals could do what they want with their teaching assistants. . . . So I was the assistant to the principal. So we set up rules. What you could do and couldn't do. You could not disrespect teachers. If you disrespected people and didn't do what you were supposed to do, you were sent to the principal. But instead of going to the principal, they went to me. Because Joe trusted me enough to make the right decisions about the kids. . . .

This school was amazingly rough. It was because they took the lily-white, up-on-the-hill school, with all the upper-middle-class White people, and mixed it with the downtown African American kids. And when these kids came up here, they were very, very powerful. There were fights. There was always name-calling. Amazing! Joe had to get the teachers to understand the racism they were putting down on these kids. Some of it was very subtle racism, but you'd see only Black kids in the hall. You wouldn't see White kids in the hall. And it infuriated him. It made him so-oo angry.

African American teachers throughout the school district shared Quakie and Elaine's admiration for Joe and his understanding of the institutional racism that pervaded its schools. They believed, as did Elaine, that "he was about giving Black kids an equal chance with the White kids." There were, however, limited numbers of certified African American teachers available. In spite of active attempts to recruit them, there were never more than 5 out of a total teaching staff of 20 during Joe's tenure at Betsy Miller. Knowing he needed a broader base of support, he began identifying teachers already at the school who shared his values and beliefs, had an interest in working for change and who could stand up to the pressures they might face from other teachers. Sandy Walden, a European American woman who came to the school from Harold Dodge, was one. In our interview, she described her initial distrust and dislike of Joe, and how she eventually came to respect him.

Sandy: Joe came. He had a vision, but I didn't like him, I really didn't like him. And I thought he hated me.

Judy: What was that about?

Sandy: I really believed in direct instruction at the time, and I still do within certain contexts and certain frameworks, but that's where I came from. Anyway, I applied for a transfer [after he came here], and a new school was opening. I thought it would be very exciting to start in a new school, start from the bottom up, and how would it be to have everybody come together and decide what a school should look like. Little did I know that was what was going to happen at Betsy Miller. And then Joe said, "I wish you would reconsider your decision for a transfer, because you're going to get it. You're going to get everything you want if you go. They'll give you the grade, they'll give you the room, they'll give you everything you want." And I said, "Why do you want me to stay?"

Judy: Interesting.

Sandy: And it was, because I didn't think he knew a thing about me. I didn't think he knew a thing about my classroom. I thought he hated me. . . . And then he came out with all these incredible things that he thought I did, and I couldn't believe it. And he said, "I would hope you would consider staying. I really want you here."

Judy: How did he know what you were doing?

Sandy: Well, I don't know, and to this day I don't know how he knows what anybody's doing, because it never seemed like he was around very much. So he's either incredibly insightful and can pick up a tremendous amount, but I just think he has an uncanny ability to do that, and to know what's happening quickly and to take a lot in, and to trust parents and children and what other people are saying. So I thought about it and thought about it, and I didn't know what to do, and I really hated Betsy Miller. It was just awful, every day was just battlegrounds.

Judy: So how long were you there at that point?

Sandy: I started in 1983. I had worked half a year at Harold Dodge, the year before it closed. I came up the year of the merger. . . . So anyway, then I said, "OK Joe. I've decided I'm going to stay." And in great Joe form, he said, "OK," and turned around and walked away. It was so funny, but I felt like that typified something about Joe, that he has a really hard time telling you you're doing a really great job, and a few times I feel like I've heard that, but in this interesting way. I know that he respects me, so much, and that if I needed anything from him, he was there. And in time of personal crisis, he was kind to me and laid off me, just like he knew that I wasn't going to take on any other committees. He knew I wasn't going to do anything else, and he never said, "How come you're not showing up?" I really appreciated that.

Anyway, so Joe came, and a lot of people left. He was a czar. He was unkind to the people who he disagreed with, and it really fell out pretty clearly who wanted to go with a forward-looking, progressive education, and who wanted the status quo, and those people left.

I don't know what made that man a great leader, I don't know. I think about that a lot. I can't quite figure it out. He is not the most articulate guy, his writing is mediocre, but I just think it's passion. It just flows from his blood, he doesn't let anything stop him, he just keeps going and he had vision up the wazoo. So all I can come up with is passion and vision, and trust. 'Cause he really trusted us, I really feel, and I felt very respected by him. After he said that he liked me and he wanted me to stay, I felt that very much.

Judy: Have you ever regretted your decision to stay?

Sandy: No, I only worry that something will happen now to change it, 'cause I couldn't teach anywhere else. No, before Joe came, I was very involved in the union, and I've been on a bunch of curriculum committees, and I was writing songs for Macmillan, the publishing company, and was doing well with that. I thought, it's such a drag I have to teach because all I really like doing is writing curriculum, but I can't do any of that unless I'm a teacher. But I wasn't really enjoying the teaching; I was actually bored sometimes. And now, I think, I don't care about any of that other stuff, I just want to be a teacher. . . . I just love being a teacher here.

Those who did leave created the opportunity for Joe to hire additional staff. Karen Shriver was among those hired in 1987 to fill a vacated position. Although he had never seen her teach, as with Sandy, Joe recognized her commitment to children and admired her feistiness. Karen told of her hiring:

I went to an interview Thursday afternoon before Labor Day with Joe Stefano, and tried to be real adamant that I didn't want to come to Betsy Miller. I wasn't interested in fourth grade. And I knew immediately when I left that's not the kind of feistiness you do with Joe, because that's what attracted him to me. And I knew when I went home, well so much for being really straightforward and honest and really clear about what I wanted, because I knew I was going to Betsy Miller. They called me the next day.

It would not be difficult for Joe to attract other teachers from among the White community. There were many highly educated, creative, and progressive women and men living in the community who were certified teachers. Some had, however, chosen not to teach in public schools. In addition to seeing schools as institutions that reinforced societal inequities, their personal experiences as teachers in public schools included being required to follow curricula and instructional mandates they neither believed in nor found effective. Many were also not willing to put up with working conditions that demanded unquestioning obedience to authoritarian administrators they did not respect. These teachers were looking for a school that was concerned with providing equitable educational programs and also valued creativity and innovation. Carol Franklin was one such teacher. She was a European American with a background in child development and social work, and had taught at the preschool and elementary levels before moving here. While teaching at two other elementary schools in this community, she had been required to use a basal reader series she found inappropriate and ineffective for her students. These experiences and others led her to question whether or not she would continue to teach in a public school. Carol explained:

I wanted to teach; with my background in social work and child development, what got me interested in teaching here was the diversity. [My friend] was here at the time, and he said, "Come work here." He was a teacher here, and had been here just a few years. So I looked, and met with Joe, and he kind of said, "Meet Belinda and Karen." And there was an opening in fourth grade, which I didn't want. I really wanted K–3, but anyway, that's how I came here. . . . And that year Karen and I decided we would work together, and we really planned all of our units together.

Their collaborations would become pivotal to the changes that were about to occur. Carol, Karen, and other teachers would provide the kind of leadership that encouraged and supported innovation by other teachers.

STARTING SIMPLE

Joe began identifying structural features he believed contributed to the chaos at the school. He consistently relied on the teacher allies he had brought to the school to convince others to give his top-down structural changes a chance to work. These actions were simple, straightforward, and pragmatic, quickly altering students' behaviors and changing their interactions with teachers and one another. Joe described two changes he made:

Behavior was a real issue, or discipline. There was a real antagonism with the downtown kids; they were angry, they were continually fighting. They were the only kids bused. I should say they were bused in addition to everything else, and they had a peculiar system of dismissing kids, particularly from the main building. All the kids went from the classrooms to the playground at the back end of the school, had to wait in line by bus number, and then had to walk up the stairs and along the street to board the bus. Well, if there was ever a setup for kids to misbehave, that was it. Because what you did was first of all you took a group of kids that were pretty active to begin with, at the end of the day you slowed them down because they had to line up. While the walkers could be dismissed, they had to line up. They had to wait for their bus to be called, and the inevitable situation ensues, where the classroom teachers don't keep track of which kids were on what bus. So, you had kids who would come down, they'd be on the wrong bus and have to be sent back. It was a comedy of errors.

Talk about a bureaucratic mess. And then there was no way to communicate with the office for the supervisors at that point. I was one of them, and later Elaine. But, in order to tell the office what buses had arrived, we had to use walkie-talkies because there was no [other] way to communicate. Well, after putting up with that for a period of time, it finally occurred to me that we could dismiss them in a much more sane and orderly way. They could just stay in their classrooms and play until the buses came. But that was symptomatic of the way we treated these kids, and then they were the object of everyone's attention, because naturally they were either fighting or pushing or shoving or doing any one of a thousand things. . . .

I also did away with a lunchroom. I found that one way to ease a whole level of supervision and to make lunch hours saner, was to have kids eat in the classroom. . . . [The reaction of teachers to that] was mixed. They did it because I said they had to basically. However, I did have some teachers come with me who could say to them, "Try it, you'll like it." And that kind of put them off a bit, and they did try it and they found that it was a much saner affair. So when I went to do something crazy like that, that was unheard of, the [teachers who knew me] could interpret it for me, and that helped. They could say, "You know, just give it a little bit of time, and you'll see that it works."

Other changes would be introduced by staff that began altering students' interactions with one another and their teachers. In 1988 a program in conflict management was introduced by one teacher that would eventually be adopted schoolwide. The processes taught to children would also become incorporated into teachers' interactions with one another. That same year Elaine Cook introduced kickball (a simplified version of baseball in which a large rubber ball is kicked instead of batted), which helped bring a new sense of order and community to Betsy Miller. Elaine's response to one teacher's resistance provides an example of how the process she used in introducing the game fostered collegiality among staff and demonstrates how respect for teacher autonomy was maintained when new initiatives were introduced:

I went to every teacher and every classroom and I said, "If you'd like to play kickball just sign this sheet of paper." They all signed up except for Martha. She wouldn't let her kids sign up because she thought it was going to be too competitive. She's the only one who, at that time, wouldn't let her kids play kickball. She said, "It will be too tough and when they come in from the playground they are going to be fighting each other." So I said, "OK, that's your choice."

So we started the league. The rules were: You cannot swear; you cannot hurt anybody; you cannot touch anybody else; you cannot throw the ball at another person; you cannot insult another person; you have to listen to the umpire. Whatever the umpire says, you cannot argue: If you're safe, you're safe; if you're out, you're out. You have to respect each person playing and the people on the sidelines. Well, Martha was right. They came in fighting. "My team was better than your team. You can't play." The whole thing. It took me 2 weeks [to change it.] . . .

Every kid who wanted [to play] was on a team. What I did was put all their names down and numbered them 1, 2, 3, 4, 5, 6 . . . 'til I had 10 teams of kids that wanted to play kickball. I had to schedule them, a different team playing a different team every day. Every day, I was the only one out there. Every day I was the umpire. I was alone out there, but a couple of teachers would come out and watch the games. Finally, what I did because I couldn't handle it by myself is that I went to the teachers and asked if they wanted to be coaches of a team. Now what this does is it gets teachers more familiar with all of the kids on all the different teams and it makes them involved with what's going on with discipline. Still, Martha wouldn't do it. Her kids got so angry. She had fourth grade and it was the toughest little fourth grade you ever did see. And she saw the other kids coming back in because they knew that the rule was you couldn't fight, couldn't yell, couldn't scream and couldn't this and couldn't that. The only thing you were allowed to do was to go out and have fun. . . .

The kids got phenomenal at kickball—unbelievable. Teachers got involved. They each had their team. Mr. B. had his team. Finally Martha gave in and said, "OK! Put my kids on the teams." She had 20 kids. So I divided them up and put them all on teams. Each team had 12–13 players and you could substitute 3. If someone got held in because they didn't get their homework done, they didn't get to play. So that changed the homework problem. The homework started coming in. A little silly game.

When the teachers got involved, they named the teams: the Red Dragons, the Mighty Mightsters. We had kids that took this so seriously that they would shovel snow off the playground to go play a game of kickball. It started in April through June, but sometimes it started in the end of March, depending on the school calendar and weather. The teachers would get out there with their teams, doing exercises, jumping up and down.

After the whole school—teachers as well as students—became involved, Elaine decided there should be an all-star team and talked it over with Joe. They came to an agreement.

Elaine: We would pick the kids that were good at kickball, good academically, good with teammates, with sportsmanship, the whole thing.
Judy: What if there was a kid who, let's say, couldn't read.
Elaine: He could still make the team. We would go to his teacher and ask, "What do you think? Does this kid deserve to be an all-star? Have you seen any change in his behavior? Have you seen any change in his academics?"
Judy: So it wasn't that he had to be at grade level or above grade level but that he was making progress?
Elaine: That's exactly how it happened. And so my brother called me. "My team [at Midtown School] is so great." No, I said, "My team is better." "So," he said, "you think yours is better?" So I said we

should have a little contest to see. So I set it up. I got permission from Joe to have a game after school, and my brother got permission from his principal. And I said, "Let's get the superintendent of schools to be the referee." So he was the second base umpire. A gym teacher from here was the umpire behind the plate; another from Midtown was the first base umpire. We got the high school football field. We bought the kids from both schools. We had transportation down, but their kids had to walk. We had a marching corps bus because my brother and I had a marching corps at the time, and my other brother drove. So he went to their school and picked up kids and took them down. We had 50 cheerleaders—everyone who didn't make the all-star team or wanted to be a cheerleader. With pom-poms and everything. This school was so hyped up in June [1989]; it was the last week of school. The local newspaper was there, and everyone could see the trophy we won—it was that high.

INSTRUCTIONAL CHANGE

By 1988 most teachers remaining at Betsy Miller shared a commitment to educational equity and believed that all children could succeed, given the correct circumstances. In this context, instructional innovations began in some classrooms and among small groups of teachers. Although it was impossible to get a trustworthy picture of the exact sequence leading to these individual innovations and collaborations, there emerged a consistent picture of a process that eventually led to instructional change throughout the school. DISTAR disappeared, basal readers were fading, and most teachers embraced whole-language approaches. Although they shared a commitment to every child's success, teachers did not always agree about pedagogy or have the same professional preparation. For example, during her first year Karen worked with Belinda Richardson, one of five African American teachers at the school in 1988. They both taught fourth grade and were committed to educational equity. Unlike Karen, however, Belinda did not object to tracking or direct instruction if done in a culturally appropriate context that maintained high expectations. Coming from an early childhood background, Karen favored child-centered developmental approaches. In spite of these differences, they decided to collaborate to create a reading program that neither could accomplish successfully by herself. This required the integration of both sets of instructional beliefs.

Belinda recalled their initial collaborations. Like other teachers, she had difficulty providing an exact sequence of events but was able to ground her recollections in interactions with specific children. This kind of child-related discourse was evident in every interview with teachers, demonstrating how children remained at the center of their thinking and practice. Belinda's recollections of her interactions with Joe demonstrate his openness to diverse initiatives proposed by teachers whose work he respected:

> The year I taught fourth grade, Karen and I worked together. There were just two of us, I think that's how it started. I think that was my first time. See, I get these mixed up because I was in fourth grade for 2 years, and I can never remember if we were together the first year or the second, but I think it was the first. It had to be. Bobby Banks—I had Bobby as a third grader, and I gave him up, because he was in a classroom with another little boy named Marcus, and they liked each other a great deal. They were great friends, but it wasn't a healthy relationship, in terms of their academics. . . .
>
> That fourth-grade year, we still had the Houghton-Mifflin series. Now I don't have a problem with the basal series, because I've never used a basal series as my total reading program. It's a resource, it's another way of getting across the skills and making sure that even if you don't cover them, you know what they are and you know where they are in some sort of continuum that makes some sense. But those kids were looking at this book for the second or third time, whatever it was. And I said, "This won't work. I won't be able to get from September to June with this class as a self-contained class. They have too many needs."
>
> And it was going to be fine, because I knew what I could do with them, but I also know how I work. I'm very intense. They were very intense, and I said, "One of us is going to burn out, and they have to come to school, so it'll be me that is outta here." So I went to Joe, and I always do this: I never go to Joe and say, "You gotta do this." I always go to him with a plan. I went and I said, "Look, this is what I'm able to do and willing to do, and put the time and effort into. I know you're not real high on this, but I'd like to split the kids out in something vaguely referred to as ability groups." I knew that was going to make him go ballistic. I knew that. But I also knew that most of the time that people talk about ability groups and they say low, that's not what you get. That's almost never what you get. . . .
>
> It was at the very beginning, in September. If it hadn't happened in September, I wouldn't have tried to do that. So we took all the kids from both the rooms and we worked out who needed to be where. And [the reading teacher] came into the room. But it all started because Bobby threw a book down on the floor and said he was not going to read that book again. It couldn't get any clearer

than that, so it went from there on. . . . What it was, was that if you're in a room with someone who's reading *Call of the Wild* as an 8- or 9-year-old, and you're just making your way through *Frog and Toad*, and you're 8 or 9, you don't want anybody to know that; so you're not going to do anything. But if you're in the room with somebody who's reading *Superfudge*, and you're reading *Frog and Toad*, "I can handle that, because I think I can get to *Superfudge*. I think I can let you know this because I think that's doable. But *Call of the Wild*, I'm never gonna get there, so I'm not doing anything at all." And that's the same way with the math, if you're working with the kids who can do algebraic equations, and you see that, and you're still struggling with your basic facts, why should you let anybody know that? So we shorten the range, and the kids who people perceive as low, unmotivated, and so on, they felt they had a shot. . . .

You've gotta be looking for the change, because the change will come. But you decide that's who this kid is and that's all they are, you won't see the change when it comes, and you're just going to keep doing what you're doing; and they'll say, "You don't know me." And that's it: they're done with you, and they're going to fulfill your every expectation.

The following year, Carol was hired as a fourth-grade teacher and joined the collaborative efforts initiated by Belinda and Karen.

Well, we just got talking. Karen was very excited at that point because she had started to do some work in author studies, what have you, and then I had some ideas to share, and we just found we bounced off each other. And it was synergistic, that we were of like mind and could support each other. So what we would do is brainstorm a unit together, and I remember we did a bunch of author studies that year. So she'd do it, and then write up stuff and ideas, and then I'd do one, and we'd trade whole units back and forth. So we really got each other going.

The success of their collaborations would start to influence other teachers who were initially opposed to using whole-language approaches with African American students. Karen explained what happened when her students entered Quakie's class the following fall as fifth graders.

They had felt so successful as readers, when they went into fifth grade and Quakie handed them a basal, they looked at her and said, "No way. We want to do reading the way Karen did reading." And these were African American children that were telling her that. So that made her really change her practice. . . .

She was so impressed that they felt so strongly about themselves that she came to me and tried to find out more about it; and she, who had really been against whole language, was more willing to get away from the basal and do some different things because these kids had quite a voice to her, and had felt pretty good about themselves the year before. So it did have effect in the school because then she started coming on board in a way that she probably wouldn't have if she hadn't heard it from children.

While this was taking place in the fourth and fifth grades, teachers at the Annex were exploring new ways of teaching math to younger students, and experimenting with integrating ESL instruction into general education classrooms. Suzanne recalled how these separate instructional initiatives came together and eventually changed teaching throughout the school.

Suzanne: What I saw happening at [the Annex] was Wendall collaborating with us [in ESL]. Also, *Math Your Way* got disseminated here. What was happening across the street was Belinda, Karen, and Carol saying that they wanted to work together and they wanted to do author studies, and this, that, and the other. And Joe's saying, "Well, how do you want to do this? When are you going to do it? What do you need to do it?"

They went and put a tremendous amount of effort into a collaboration and someplace in the middle of the year, January or February, some terrible snowy night, they gave a presentation on what they were doing. And it was this great collaboration, this great thing that they had come up with, the three of them, that came out of their collaboration.

Judy: Were there any skeptics in all this—people who just didn't participate?

Suzanne: Well, yeah, but if you had Karen and Carol and Belinda so thrilled with what they had done, you had three people walking around going ha ha ha ha ha, and you wanted a piece of it. You had Wendall and me and Julie walking around going ha ha ha ha ha ha. And so, "Hey, I want a piece of that. Let's do it." . . . So people were doing that the next year, and it got to be almost the whole school doing it that way, and those people who weren't doing it that way were leached out. And we started doing a lot of whole language, and people who weren't doing it that way were nudged out.

What moved teachers was neither the theoretical soundness of any one approach nor validation from scientifically based research. Rather, as Joe explained, it was "the actual experience; the recognition that these kids who were traditionally sent out, could in fact participate." Joe described the process of change in terms of the whole school this way:

> A critical mass began to see the legitimacy of these approaches. As more and more people jumped over, in a sense, then it became part of the culture. Because at first it would be a radical idea, and gradually as they either saw it working with other people, their colleagues, or as they saw it working for themselves, then they began to see the change in behavior. The single most [important] selling point of all of that was these very kids that were the object of everybody's attention, their behavior was being modified, because these kids now had an investment in the school and in the classroom. . . .
>
> But the thing that was most important was that the teachers began to recognize that whatever they did had to be somewhat open-ended, and had to take into account that you had this range of kids that had to be part of the whole; and unless you made them part of the whole, you couldn't really continue on. That was a two-way sword, because the minute you start opening it up like that, the parents of the kids who were traditionally on top are going to say to you, "Well, my kid isn't being enriched." So the challenge got even greater for the teachers, particularly the intermediate-level teachers— Karen and Carol and Belinda. They had to show that they could provide enough stimulation and intellectual rigor so that those kids were sufficiently challenged.
>
> This meant that the program had to change, because the way it was constructed, these kids that we're talking about were on the outside looking in. We started to rethink, and I think one of the things that helped, there were enough people on staff who were willing to say this is a problem, and we need to do something about it. And they were at least willing to consider some ideas.

PROGRAMMATIC CHANGE

Low family income and poor academic performance among the children from Harold Dodge had increased the number of students eligible to receive support services at Betsy Miller. Although the school district supplied the required number of specialists for these children and for those with limited English language skills, the model that had been in place to deliver these services was clearly ineffective. Support was provided to individuals or in small groups of children outside the general education classroom; these teacher specialists and related service providers rarely collaborated with classroom teachers. Their charge was to remedy deficits and help children reach annual goals and short-term objectives set by the school district's Committee on Special Education. Some children who had been classified as eligible for special education services received support in one of two resource rooms. Most were African American boys classified as having learning disabilities and/or emotional and behavioral disorders that had either been at Harold Dodge or would have been there had the schools not merged. Their instruction was not directly connected to what went on in classrooms. Joe explained:

> So you had this continual movement of children, which impacted every single classroom in the school, and the problem resulted in the classroom teachers never having a class together. There was either a group coming or going, or somewhere in between. . . . The first thing we tackled were the services. The immediate problem being, how do we hang on to our kids so we have some semblance of classroom community, on some consistent basis.

Changing the way support was provided became central to keeping kids in classrooms. Although Joe identified this as "the first thing we tackled," teacher-initiated programs such as conflict resolution, kickball, and informal collaborations were simultaneously creating a context that made programmatic and instructional change possible. Rachel Meyer, the special education support teacher during Joe's administration, was central to developing a new way of providing support services. She described the change process leading to the blended services model as evolving naturally: "We said we were very organic, we just kept growing." Her story provides another example of how teachers' commitments to children were at the heart of the school's culture. It also illustrates the empowering impact of Joe's encouragement and support.

Rachel: My title was "support teacher." But the responsibility of my job was as a chairperson of the building Committee on Special Education, and I was supposed to do all of the initial diagnostic work, the academic diagnostic work for any kind of classification or any child who came through the support team. I was also the chair of the support team, and I was supposed to coordinate the school psychologist, and the speech and language person; all of the specialists.

Judy: And all the schools had a person in that role?

Rachel: Yes, all the schools had them. Of course, they had very different populations. Some people who had my job sat in their offices, and were able to really do some of the things that I never got around to, like being a true resource for the classroom teacher. There were so many pieces to my job. And I came in and I said to Joe, "I'm so fragmented, I can't do my job. I can no longer sit here and see children who are really being pulled in so many different directions, and they're not making progress. They're really not. Everyone has good intentions, and the specialists are very skilled and very knowledgeable, and everyone is trying, but [kids] go back to the classroom [they were taken out of] even for a brief amount of time, and everything has passed them by. There's nothing that they can do to practice all of these skills that we are trying to help them with in the resource room, or in the Title I room, it's crazy."

And then I said, "I can't do my job anymore." And I remember I left, and I pulled over to the side of the road on the way home because I was crying so much. I just could not go back home. And I said, "I have to get another job, I can't do this." I think that was on a weekend, and I came back on Monday, and Joe said, "I've been thinking about what you said, and I agree with you."

And it was just fortunate that my feelings and then Joe's real support of my feelings were really mirrored by other staff members. Not everyone, but there were a lot of people on the staff who felt similarly. Once I got out there to be explicit enough, and not just me; when we were able to talk about the craziness of what was happening to our kids.

Judy: So two questions. What was the vehicle for talking? And what percentage of teachers do you think felt the way you did?

Rachel: A core of teachers felt that way, but it wasn't 50%. . . . The whole idea that we were really looking at doing possibly something else because this just wasn't working, and the something else was very amorphous. We didn't know what we were gonna do. We knew that what we were doing wasn't working. And the specialists, some of the specialists knew that too, but yet they felt that they wanted to do their job. The resource room teacher had a big responsibility to fill all those IEPs, and there I was meeting with Title I reading teachers.

We were going through long-term and short-terms goals for these kids, and we were putting them all on paper. And you know, it was a wonderful exercise theoretically, but practically, the kids were just not doing well. I think the most dramatic way they weren't doing well, they were very misbehaved. They were all over the place. There was nothing really appropriate for them in the classroom. They're very smart, and they have lots of energy, and they want very much to be engaged. So they engage themselves in the most incredible activities. It was just clear, their naughtiness had to do with the fact that their needs were not being met, not academically, not emotionally.

Judy: So, you talked to Joe; you weren't happy; there were a bunch of other unhappy people. You said the staff began to talk about this stuff. How did that start to happen?

Rachel: Joe, Karen, and I went to a conference to make a presentation about how we all worked together, and we started to talk about how we really weren't working together. And everyone was very conscientious and doing their bit, but not really in any kind of collaborative way, or congruent way. And so we talked a lot on the way home.

Joe's recollection of what happened next illustrates both the organic nature of the programmatic changes that followed and the way he negotiated bureaucratic rules and regulations to make things happen.

So we started playing around with the notion of putting the specialists in the classrooms rather than sending the kids to the specialists. And that evolved over a couple of years. We started with ESL folks. . . . We got teachers to volunteer to get some ESL training through a grant one of the ESL teachers actually had gotten. They did some work in the summer and once a month they went out and learned ESL teaching techniques, the classroom teachers along with ESL teachers.

And what that began to do was to institutionalize the notion that these kids could be taught in the mainstream, that the teachers would coteach rather than teach individually. And that started us down the path of collaboration and in-class services. So then the following year, we looked to doing Title I teachers and special ed teachers. Now the big problem there was that there are sort of unwritten rules that if you were a special ed teacher you couldn't teach a Title I kid and if you were a Title I teacher you certainly couldn't teach special ed kids. Well, those were rules that were made mainly by us. While there is some regulation that might have gotten in the way, I took the position that what the hell's the difference? As long as you don't subvert the intent of the service, whether you're a Title I teacher or a special ed teacher, if you can teach, you can teach. . . . For years everyone swore up and down that only special ed teachers could teach classified kids special ed math. Well, that was nonsense. What the regulation said, it was pretty clear, that if you wrote it on the IEP it had to be a particular need that had to be met; as long as you could show that you were meeting it, there really wasn't much anybody could do about that. So that was partly how I got around it. I mean I did understand the idea that you can't subvert the intent of the service and nullify the use of the money. You don't take the money and supplement the district budget. You take the money and make sure the kid gets the service.

By putting teachers in classes for a longer period of time, most of the kids got more. For instance, the old rule used to be that Title I kids had to get 90 additional minutes of instruction over the course of the week. Well, the minute I put somebody in the classroom, at say, half-time, the kid had far more exposure to the Title I teacher and the classroom teacher for that matter. And when you look at it that way, not only was the instruction integrated, but there could be more focus in a more particular way because now you had one and a half teachers as opposed to one teacher who was responsible for everything and everybody.

All pull-out services would be eliminated by 1992. Although teachers supported this decision, some continued to believe that there were some children who needed more systematic instruction in a less distracting environment than was possible in a general education classroom. Some of these teachers would transfer to other schools. Those remaining would be willing to give it a try and stick with the program as long as they believed children's needs were being met. The teachers that stayed may have disagreed with some surface practices but continued to share deeper cultural commitments. They valued their relationships with colleagues and wanted to be part of a school in which caring for children was central. These teachers would continue to have an important role in maintaining the dynamic tension between collective ideology and individual needs and concerns that became central to Betsy Miller's culture, but was rarely found in other public schools.

CHAPTER 5

Deepening Cultural Commitments

In 1992, consultants from the Prospect Center for Education and Research were asked to evaluate the outcome of the change process that took place at Betsy Miller between 1987 and 1992. Through an analysis of extensive interviews with staff, parents, and children from Betsy Miller, and systematic observations at the school, the authors of the study concluded that the goals identified by staff had been met. These goals included the following:

- To form a community, and to do that by generating an atmosphere of inclusion and respect for the individual and by valuing diversity in the school, making it a focus for celebration
- To ensure that the school is comfortable and safe enough for children, teachers, and parents to feel they can take the risks fundamental to learning and growing
- To act in accordance with the belief that *all* children can learn and, given an environment that values individuals, will become self-directed learners and independent thinkers able to advocate for their own educations
- To offer a program that recognizes the interwovenness of knowledge and strives to keep it whole through an interdisciplinary approach to curriculum

The researchers presented evidence of these accomplishments in a case study report, describing what they found to be central to reaching these goals. They identified the impetus for change as having come from the staff's recognition of the need to respond to the diversity that characterized the school after the merger with Harold Dodge. The authors put it this way: "It was diversity that brought about a serious commitment to inclusion. It was diversity and attention to inclusion that transformed the way the school works." This transformation began with teacher's acknowledgement that the fundamental structure of the school was flawed. During these

5 years, the school would move from being a place where teachers and children worked in isolation from one another to one where "cooperation and collaboration defined the learning and social program for children."

These changes led to outcomes for children that evaluators from the Prospect Center described as "nothing less than profound." In their final written report to the school they stated:

> Most simply, [Black and White] parents and teachers are no longer deeply worried as they once were about the children and their safety. Going beyond that, the condition of the children is, in fact, a measure of the vitality and the appropriateness of the social and learning environment provided by the school.

The report provided parents' and teachers' descriptions of the impact of the school on children's learning in terms of students' growing enthusiasm and involvement in what went on at the school. One parent put it this way: "The way they think, the way they look at the world, makes it clear they are excited about learning." Other parents talked about their children's work as "amazing and awe-inspiring."

The study acknowledged the significance of programmatic and organizational changes for increasing children's motivation and achievement. Its authors also recognized and emphasized that what took place at Betsy Miller between 1987 and 1992 required much more than structural change. Shared commitments to the kind of changes that were to occur were also essential. The collegiality that emerged among Betsy Miller's staff reflected a shared "world view," characterized by "patience, civility, open-mindedness, supportiveness of others, and appreciation for both likeness and difference." This "cast of mind" balanced collective needs with individual interests and concerns. The report describes Betsy Miller as operating from:

> a world view that values independence and self-regard. . . . it is appropriate [here] to question and wonder, to think for yourself, to express your ideas and make your own decisions, to believe you have something to contribute to the world (just as the world has much to offer you), and to listen and be heard by others. . . .
>
> Briefly in the first 5 years attention was concentrated on creating a very particular kind of learning and social climate for children. That climate is describable in several ways: as one in which diversity has positive value; as one in which each person and learner has membership and access; and one in which the school community is premised on cooperation and collaboration among children.

AN ORGANIC PROCESS

What follows is an analysis of how that climate emerged, through an exploration of key events identified by the staff as central to deepening their commitment to creating a culture of inclusion. As I spoke with people and reviewed archival materials, what became clear was that the relationships teachers developed during early informal collaborations were as important to their work as the content of the specific activities in which they had engaged. When describing formal staff development programs and meetings, there was never consistent agreement among teachers about which events were most vital, but all agreed that collaborative processes and shared commitments were central to promoting deep levels of cultural change. Teachers always described events in the context of their interactions and relationships with other staff, children, and parents. It was within these contexts that they became receptive to substantive change. Rachel Meyer, the special education support teacher, put it this way:

I can't really capture the whole dynamic of what happened. . . . There was a whole ethos that really is indescribable. It's almost very existential. You know, it happened, and we really did some wonderful things, but to go back and describe it or reconstruct it is very hard. I can tell you the details, but the whole spirit of it and the way that people interacted with each other; it's really very difficult.

A picture emerged of what she and others referred to as an "organic process," emphasizing that the school was still "in process." The qualitative nature of their recollections mirrored what other researchers report as central to significant organizational change.

- It was a process, not an event.
- It was accomplished by individuals.
- It was highly personal.
- It involved developmental growth.
- It was understood and described in operational terms.
- It required facilitation. (Hord, Rutherford, Huling-Austin, & Hall, 1987, pp. 5–6)

STAFF DEVELOPMENT

Teachers' awareness of the importance of "process" began in 1989 when Joe organized staff development programs to encourage group problem solving. At staff meetings, brainstorming and small-group work led to prioritizing concerns, planning, and building consensus. By 1992 these meetings were both providing information and consistently employing these processes, encouraging and supporting active engagement by the entire staff. Initially, Joe set agendas that focused on what Karen called "bigger issues." At times whole-staff meetings took place after school hours or on weekends, with either a dish-to-pass dinner or a meal Joe provided. Regardless of their time, place, or content, all meetings engaged teachers in collaborative processes.

While some staff development programs included workshops that focused on specific content (e.g., curriculum and instruction in literacy, mathematics, thematic instruction; English as a second language), others focused exclusively on process (e.g., consensus building, problem solving, and conflict resolution). The Coalition of Essential Schools, Northeast Regional Laboratory, and Prospect Center for Education and Research were called upon for information, support, and consultation. Small groups of teachers attended workshops offered by these and other organizations and presented what they learned to the entire staff. The information they provided initiated additional collaborations among teachers within teaching teams, as participants on planning committees or on task forces designed to address specific concerns. Teachers who became involved in these efforts met with one another after school, on evenings, and on weekends.

Initially, the same teachers seemed to be participating in everything, generating what some saw as an in-group. No one denied that was the case, and, in fact, some of those interviewed described themselves in that way. Karen, for example, explained that talking to her would only provide an understanding of what was happening among those teachers at the "cutting edge." It would take several years before everyone else came "on board." For new ideas to be dispersed throughout the school, innovations needed to be seen as more than the implementation of Joe's agenda or activities that represented a cadre of teacher-leaders. Sandy Walden, another teacher who became very involved in staff development, struggled to recall the exact sequence of events that led to the eventual coming together of the entire staff. She was, however, very clear about the processes they went through:

> First Joe really sent a few people [to conferences]. I was in the "in crowd." I went, and then eventually everybody went. He'd sort of say, "Has everybody been to a workshop or to an event," and people started getting excited and talking about it, and then we started meeting for math meetings; once a week we got together. And that's

where the grade-level meetings, that's where the collegiality started to change and shift and we started, I think, around math. We started really depending on each other in ways that all of a sudden, math didn't really happen very much if we didn't have those math meetings. And it was hard to think about math without thinking with our colleagues, because the thinking was so different once we brought it all together.

"Bringing it all together" would not be as hard as it was in the first 5 years. As the Prospect researchers had noted, a climate had been established by 1992 that was characteristically collaborative. Consensus now needed to develop among staff regarding which values and beliefs were most central to the school's identity.

REVISITING RACISM

As teachers came together around curriculum and personal relationships deepened, discussions began including race and racism. White teachers were becoming sensitized to their own racism through personal relationships with African American teachers. This led several White teachers to participate in courses and workshops on racism and bring what they learned back to the entire staff. Elaine Cook's advocacy for African American students and outreach to their families was also heightening awareness and developing better relationships between teachers and African American families.

Parents and staff interviewed during the Prospect Center's evaluation of the school's progress had voiced general satisfaction with the direction the school had taken since 1987. African American parents felt their children were safe, and appropriate learning opportunities were being provided. Most recognized, however, that more needed to be done to prepare their children to face racism in this community and elsewhere. Acknowledging that their concerns extended beyond the school, parents and staff concurred that a more serious examination of racism was needed if the school was to be truly inclusive in how it prepared students for life in the community.

Responding to these concerns led staff to initiate a series of workshops in January of 1993 called "Revisiting Racism." A representative committee of teachers approached faculty members at the local university whose professional interest focused on working with organizations to counteract institutional racism. Working collaboratively, teachers and consultants identified the following two primary objectives for a workshop series:

- Continue working to understand personal and institutional racism so racist practices can be transformed at Betsy Miller Elementary School.
- Discuss and recommend changes in school policies that perpetuate racism.

Workshop sessions took place once a month in the evening from January through May 1993, and were facilitated by university faculty. The entire staff, including paraprofessionals, and a representative group of parents participated. Although many activities followed processes most staff had used before (small-group work, brainstorming, sharing ideas, and developing consensus), a good deal of time was spent explaining and exploring process concerns. Process observers were assigned to report on positive and negative aspects of group interactions, including silencing any individuals across or within groups. To help create a safe place for exploring personal racism, small groups were separated by race, creating an all African American group.

During the first session, each small group was asked to generate lists answering two questions that were the focus of the workshops. These lists were then combined, discussed and synthesized into a final list all could agree upon. Consensus was reached quickly on the wording of the list that answered the first question, "What has Betsy Miller accomplished toward transforming racism in the last 3 to 5 years?" The combined list read as follows:

1. Teachers are continuously working on issues.
2. Most kids seem comfortable here; many are empowered.
3. Inclusive groupings of kids within their classroom.
4. Changes in the way we deal with special education kids; much less sorting and labeling.
5. Tenor of the school, for example, comments by a visitor, "These kids act like they own the school."
6. Adults seriously attempting to work as a community; principal and/or group of staff don't fear the need to intervene when there is intense discussion. [There is] serious commitment on part of most staff to work together.
7. Acceptance of people for what they are; shift of focus from what's wrong with people, looking at who they are.
8. We are focused on what's best for kids.
9. Talking it out instead of physical fighting.
10. Cooperative learning over competition.

11. Sense of individual worth and needs—goal setting. Individual investment in learning.
12. Process-based, whole-language writing process.

Race, racism, or multicultural education were not listed. Instead, Black and White, staff and parents, all understood how structures, programs, and practices that had evolved at Betsy Miller by 1993 were supported by beliefs and values that combated institutional racism.

Answers to the second question, "What areas need further work in order to transform racism?" would prove more difficult to agree upon. Tension emerged when the African American group presented its recommendations. In addition to pointing out the discomfort they sometimes felt when interacting with White staff, African Americans expressed a lack of trust and a sense that they did not belong to a shared community with some of their White colleagues. They also believed communication with many African American families was still inadequate, leading to parental misunderstandings about what the school was trying to accomplish. Although progress had been made, too many of their children were still victims of what some called *institutional sorting*, that is, labeling and identification for remedial and special education services. They believed African American children needed opportunities to be with only other African American children while at school. This would help students feel safe and supported in talking about issues inhibiting their learning, including those related to racism.

By the end of the third session, the entire staff agreed to implement the following three recommendations for change.

1. All students at Betsy Miller Elementary School will participate in *family groups*. Family groups will be organized by race.
2. Betsy Miller will create an immersion model for classroom grouping of African American children similar to the ESL model.
3. All African American children will be off Title I by 1995.

The following, taken from a written summary of these meetings, explains the thinking of African American staff and parents who were advocating for some time for their children to be with one another:

One of the ways that racism is perpetuated in education is through subtle and overt institutional norms that avoid open discussions on racism. This form of repression says to young people, "Racism is a topic we don't talk about." This norm impacts on all the students regardless of race and clearly reinforces denial and avoidance, which is an insidious way to perpetuate racism without looking racist.

... The isolation of African American students from one another is another way to maintain silence on racism, to limit their race identity as a group, and to limit their success in school.

... Separate groups will help create the norm, "We want you to talk about racism in a safe environment so we can all unlearn racism." It will, of course, be very important for White staff to feel comfortable talking about unlearning their own racism.

The following statement written by a White teacher reflects the shared understanding that developed among both Black and White teachers that led to adopting the recommendation for family groups and immersion for African American students:

Self-determination is an essential action for any oppressed group. Women know how different our lives would be if not for women-only groups, courses, services, and so on. Those WOMEN ONLY signs made men nervous—they feared loss of controlling us. So it is for White people when people of color organize themselves exclusive of us.

When any group's cultural identity has been hidden and "whited out" systematically by another group through institutions (like school), that group must find a way to reestablish itself. A sense of history, identity, and pride is essential equipment for all children. Public schools have always provided it for most European American children. We need to make our school a place where this happens for all kids. As White teachers we can do some of this in our classrooms as they are.

But we must make room for a cohesive African [American] community to develop here; to not give our blessings to some form of a school within a school is to continue the old divide and conquer approach. If our African [American] colleagues believe this is a needed step, they have my support. Leaders in their fields from Martin Luther King Jr. to Spike Lee attended all-Black schools or colleges at some point in their lives.

White people have been running schools for a long time. Our track record for children of color is dismal. Enough said.

Family groups were to be formed by grade level. Time was to be set aside each week to allow African American children to meet with one another and discuss concerns they might not otherwise feel comfortable sharing in a racially heterogeneous group. Immersion was to be organized by clustering small groups of African American children in classrooms in the same way that the ESL immersion model had placed children who spoke the same language in the same classroom whenever possible. A teacher explained this idea in the following way:

> Then the thinking evolved to include African American children. We had quite a few African American staff members at the time. The thinking was that African American staff members could preteach children concepts about their culture that would be transmitted to the rest of the class. So, for example, these children went out and learned about Kwanzaa and then we were supposed to all do Kwanzaa with the African American children taking a leadership role in the lesson.

To be certain that every African American child had at least one peer in his or her classroom, race became one of the variables considered when placing children in a class. Attempts to create family groups and an African American immersion program began but were inconsistent and intermittent. I saw no evidence of their existence during the years I visited the school. The third recommendation, the elimination of Title I programs, would also not be realized. That proposal was made as a political statement by teachers who understood the kind of radical transformation of the public education system it required. One teacher articulated the dilemmas they faced by accepting Title I support:

> If we do a good job of teaching, we will get kids off the Title I roles and lose our funding. Then we can't do the job we need to do because staffing will have to be cut back. Then when we can't teach well because of high child:adult ratios, kids will then get back into Title I and—bingo—the funding is back and we can do a good job again.
>
> If we refuse to cooperate with a fundamentally racist and class-biased sorting system, we lose our funding. Title I is *designed* to keep X percent of our kids labeled *deficient.*
>
> Can we root out personal and institutional racism at Betsy Miller and still cooperate with a program like Title I? I think at some point we need to take a stand and reorganize ourselves accordingly. . . . It's a struggle that has to go beyond Betsy Miller.

The recommendation to eliminate Title I programs represented a commitment to reducing failure among African American children. To do this, staff agreed to continue examining the impact of their own views of children on their teaching practices; commit to high levels of achievement among all students; maintain or increase the size of the school's staff; continue to advocate for children when they graduated from Betsy Miller. These ideals would be sustained even though the programmatic recommendations of the workshops were never fully realized. The processes modeled by the workshop organizers would also continue to be used in staff interactions with one another, parents, and students.

The racism workshops were remembered by staff as strengthening interracial relationships, coalescing resolve to combat racism, and leading to a schoolwide declaration that Betsy Miller was a bias-free zone. Staff awareness of the relationship between empowerment and their ability to effect change was also heightened. The following statement taken from the summary report of the workshop continues to resonate in the way Betsy Miller teachers talk about their school: "The most important and resistant step in the process of transforming racism [are] changes that directly challenge the unequal distribution of power. Access to knowledge and skills is a form of power."

PILOT PROJECTS

School Restructuring

Teachers would continue developing their knowledge and skills throughout the early 1990s. This was the era when they believed anything was possible and could not imagine teaching anywhere else. By 1992 teachers were empowered, receptive to new ideas, and fired with possibility. They would design staff development programs funded by the school district and supported by a progressive State Department of Education. The school district had become interested in developing and disseminating *pilot* programs that increased academic performance and addressed inequities among students throughout the district. Betsy Miller teachers would take the lead in developing these kinds of programs.

The first of these pilots led to institutionalizing schoolwide support for children in classrooms through the blended services model. This approach built on what teachers had learned through collaborations that began with ESL instruction at the Annex and, by 1992, were being implemented among scattered teams of teachers throughout the school. The 1992–93 "Pilot for School Restructuring" funded outside consultants and provided classroom coverage to enable teachers to meet with one another for developing collaborative teaching strategies to be used throughout the school. Teachers would observe and critique one another to help assure congruence and program continuity between the classroom curriculum and individual children's learning objectives.

Joe Stefano submitted the grant proposal for the pilot, but it represented the work of the entire staff. The language used in the proposal reflects the collaborative processes to be used in carrying out the project and institutionalizing change. Words and phrases demonstrating the deep commitment to collaboration have been italicized here:

A highly diverse student population and its myriad needs have caused *us* to reflect on what changes can better serve *our school* goals.

The Betsy Miller *staff has engaged in the process* of examining teaching practices, delivery of services, and school organizational structures over the past 4 years.

We have come to the conclusion that the traditional model of one teacher and a number of support specialists trying to collaboratively develop a congruent instructional program no longer meet *our needs.* Too little planning time, frequent schedule interruptions, and support staff cutbacks are fragmenting *our efforts.*

We need to expand the *collaborative model* so that the classroom teachers and support personnel can *share* the primary responsibility for the instructional program. *Our* increased knowledge of the teaching and learning processes suggests that concentrating the responsibility with the classroom teacher and having the support personnel fitting in individual classroom programs is no longer a viable model. *A team of professionals* working with a small pupil:teacher ratio on a *co-equal* basis appears to have greater potential for meeting student needs. *Collaborative planning and teaching* can be better achieved where professional staff are committed to *working together* in a more flexible organizational pattern. In addition, *our* curricular efforts also need to be expanded to create multileveled thematic units that can meet a diversity of needs.

We propose a more flexible staffing model that would remove labels from classrooms, ESL, special education (speech and resource room), and Title 1, creating *teams of professionals* that would deliver instructional services in a *collaborative, integrated* fashion.

Whole School Pilots

The work during the initial pilot was described as the "beginning of teachers' coming together as a whole school to reconceptualize their understanding of children and schooling." In the spring of 1993, five more proposals were submitted to the school district for funding additional staff and whole-school development projects. The ideas for these projects emerged through teacher collaborations that took place during the initial pilot. This time Joe's cover letter included the following statement:

> It is important to note that while my name appears on each proposal a committee of teachers did the actual work. The ideas contained in the proposals are familiar to the entire staff and reflect their support.
>
> We will collectively, as an entire staff, assume and divide up the responsibilities to implement the numerous proposals we have submitted.

Written by groups of teachers, the 1993–94 pilots were designed to create and develop the following items:

1. A quality review process as an alternative model for supervision
2. Authentic assessment models for mathematics
3. An alternative educational program with an Afrocentric focus
4. The integration of antibias and conflict mediation skills and attitudes into language arts and social studies curriculums
5. Parent-school collaborations focusing on increasing participation among African American and ESL communities

Each program was funded and preliminary work was initiated during the spring and summer of 1993.

During my years at the school, many examples of activities that developed from these projects were evident. All would continue to some degree, in some classrooms, and among small groups of teachers. The blended services model and the narrative assessment process were developed by staff through these pilot projects. Both became institutionalized, reflecting a schoolwide commitment to inclusion as a response to student diversity. This commitment was described in the 1993 evaluation report completed by consultants from the Prospect Center:

> At Betsy Miller, inclusion means and demands much more than passive membership or not being excluded. Rather, as we understand it, a very high value is placed on ownership, contribution, and active participation in the school. Indeed, it would seem to us that at Betsy Miller these values define inclusion.

AUTHENTIC ASSESSMENT

Written summaries of events that took place at Betsy Miller from 1987 through 1992 document the central role of assessment in its restructuring.

As teachers moved away from basal readers, they began incorporating anecdotal records to assess children's reading. In 1989, math assessments began including analyses of children's rough work, math journals, and interviews with children to determine conceptual knowledge. The following year, self-assessment, peer evaluations, and conferencing were added as assessment processes for both students and staff. These processes reflected ideas teachers had presented to one another from their work with the Northeast Regional Laboratory and the Prospect Archive and Center for Education and Research.

Descriptive Review

During the summer of 1992 the entire staff participated in a 2-day assessment workshop. Pat Carini, cofounder of the Prospect Center, guided teachers in recording observations of children's work and behavior, focusing on strengths and potentialities. Teachers then volunteered to present their observations in small study groups with other teachers, following a process called *descriptive review* (Carini, 2001; Himley & Carini, 2000). This process directed teachers toward examining the way values and assumptions shaped their understanding of children and demonstrated the power of sharing perspectives with colleagues through respectful interactions.

Descriptive review is more than an assessment technique: it represents a way of perceiving children and designing "learning to the learner" (Himley & Carini, 2000, p. 9). The following description, taken from documents describing the assessment workshops at Betsy Miller, illustrates the multiple facets of teaching and learning that teachers explored while applying this process.

> We will be deepening our knowledge of children, learning to be mutually responsible and interdependent in our teams, breaking new ground in the inclusion of parents in the teaching equation, and involving the children themselves as agents of their own learning.
>
> As we work things out together, we will document what is happening in the lives of children, in the lives of staff, and in the relationships of parents to the ongoing endeavor. There will be some difficult times, but we are launched on an exciting effort to implement a school with a human history, a school with stories, memories, inclusivity, and caring.

The summer workshop would have a significant impact on all dimensions of the school's culture. Collegiality would be enhanced through the shared commitments articulated by staff. The following, written by a teacher attending the workshop, offers insight into these shared values:

> We are clear about what we value as a staff. We will be learning what the children value, and what it is parents value. In working for the inclusion of the voices of all children in our teaching, boundaries will be reworked as we stop labeling children and as teachers—classroom, support, and special teachers—[begin] working together.

Primary-level commitments to compassionate care were becoming solidified among the staff.

The Narrative Assessment Process

The 1994 summer assessment workshop provided a shared experience that became the foundation for developing the narrative reporting system used throughout the school year to assess the progress of every child. As with other staff development initiatives at Betsy Miller, its impact would be broader and deeper than the practice it initiated. Relationships among staff were enhanced in ways that promoted deeper levels of collaboration. Grade-level instructional teams (K–1; 2–3; 4–5) would be formed. This would lead "specialists" to become "collaborators" assigned to teams and working in classrooms alongside lead teachers. Instructional teams would "integrate the work of support and special teachers into the curriculum planning." The workshop would also impact on the role of administrators, who became identified as *enablers* participating in team meetings and adding valuable information about children and families whenever possible. Parental involvement would also increase. A schoolwide parent meeting would be scheduled for early in the year to share plans that emerged from the workshop and solicit input from parents. Special attention would be given to assure that meetings with parents took place at sites and times convenient for all segments of the parent population.

A committee of teachers and administrators presented a proposal to the entire staff in September. After some modifications, the Pilot Project on Authentic Assessment was presented to parents, approved, and sent on to the school district. That project would lead to the development of the narrative assessment process used to assess every child at Betsy Miller. Children's progress would be evaluated by determining the degree to which the child had reached goals established by parents, teachers, and the child in a face-to-face meeting at the beginning of the year. These goals were determined collaboratively, aligning a child's strengths, interests, and experiences with parental concerns and curricular objectives. Teachers wrote a narrative summary, documenting what was agreed upon at the meeting. Parents, teachers, and children met again at midyear to evaluate progress and, at times, establish new goals. Another written report, describing each child's progress, was prepared at the end of the year, and miniconferences were held with those children and parents continuing with the same teacher for another year.

The narrative assessment process reflected deep levels of caring and respect for children that existed at the primary level of Betsy Miller's culture. Pat Carini (2001) describes these values as

> spacious and inclusive. I insist on this wide embrace because without it, as parents, educators and citizens, we find ourselves condemned to an ever narrowing definition of normalcy—in society and in the schools. If only a few children are normal and capable, it does not take great social or political acuity to guess which children and whose will be favored. (p. 15)

CHAPTER 6

Sustaining Change: An Oxymoron

In 1995 the district superintendent asked Joe to leave Betsy Miller and become principal of Midtown Elementary School. Midtown served the largest percentage of low-income African American students in the school district and, in 1995, was its lowest performing school. The superintendent was the first African American to serve in this position and recognized Joe's commitment to combating racism. He believed Joe's leadership was central to the transformation of Betsy Miller from a dysfunctional school to one that successfully addressed the social exclusion of children of color, non-English speakers, and others identified as having special educational needs. Joe agreed to move on, hoping to achieve what he had at Betsy Miller in the few years left before his retirement.

The decision to leave Betsy Miller was not easily made. Joe was deeply concerned with whether or not Betsy Miller's teachers could sustain the practices and structures they had developed collectively. Although motivated by the challenges he would face at Midtown, he felt his work at Betsy Miller was not complete and so maintained an active role at both schools. In doing so, he failed to consider or didn't fully realize how much of what he had accomplished at Betsy Miller grew out of the relationships he had established with teachers and the collective leadership that emerged. Not recognizing the importance of teacher leadership and collaboration would, in fact, interfere with establishing positive relationships with teachers at Midtown. Ignoring the unique history and context of that school, he tried to create another Betsy Miller. His efforts to impose reforms from one context to the other would be resisted by many Midtown teachers, leading to racial and interpersonal conflicts and ending long-standing friendships. Everyone I spoke with believed the stress, frustration, and disappointment that Joe experienced at Midtown, and his continuing concern for Betsy Miller contributed to his sudden heart attack and death the following year.

During his first year at Midtown (1995–96), Joe split his time between both schools, and Belinda Richardson, an African American teacher-leader at Betsy Miller, became its acting principal. The next year, 1996, an African American woman was hired as Betsy Miller's new principal and Joe became full-time principal of Midtown. That same year, the African American superintendent who had supported Joe and the reforms at Betsy Miller left the district and was replaced by a more conservative White woman. Leadership at the State Department of Education also changed. A newly elected Republican governor replaced a progressive Democrat and appointed a Commissioner of Education whose charge included developing and implementing a uniform set of statewide standards and a high-stakes testing program for all elementary school students.

Having just completed my first year observing Karen's classroom, I saw Joe's departure as an opportunity to examine the sustainability of Betsy Miller's inclusive culture in the absence of the person identified as its leader, during a time when the climate surrounding both local and state educational reforms were shifting from a focus on equity to one of accountability. Like Joe, I hadn't yet grasped the significance of teachers' collegial commitments, relationships with one another, and deep levels of caring to the school's development. At that moment, I was incapable of seeing the significance of teachers' leadership beyond their classroom practice. What took place during the next 3 years would open my eyes to the powerful possibilities of teacher collaboration and collegiality in developing and sustaining this and other schools. I would also discover the limits of teachers' power within a bureaucratic and politicized educational system.

SUSTAINING A VISIBLE-TECHNICAL DIMENSION OF A CULTURE OF INCLUSION: THE NARRATIVE ASSESSMENT PROCESS

Joe's immediate concerns for Betsy Miller centered on the 1996 districtwide requirement that all elementary schools use a uniform reporting system to document attainment of a uniform set of standards for kindergarten through second-grade students. The new report card reflected the shifts in education policy from concerns regarding equity to accountability. Although federal and state regulations continued to mandate racial integration and the inclusion of children with special educational needs in general education settings, newer reforms focused on establishing standards and monitoring student performance. The new superintendent appointed in 1996 believed that imposing more rigorous standards would compel schools to improve their scores on statewide standardized tests. She described Betsy Miller's past performance as among the poorest in the district. She did not consider, however, that although it had the largest number of non-English-speaking children and the second largest population of minority children from low-income families, it had a smaller percentage of children classified for special education and Title I reading programs than other schools in the district with similar populations.

The relationship between reading scores and the number of students receiving special education services was significant. In 1996, test scores of classified children were not averaged with others in determining a school's composite score on standardized tests. Because all children could be served in regular classrooms through the blended-services model, students who might have been identified as mildly handicapped at other schools were generally not referred for special education services at Betsy Miller. Not identifying children as in need of special education penalized the school by lowering its composite score on statewide standardized tests. Teachers' understanding of the relationship between special education and remedial services with institutional racism, along with their deep conviction that the deficit-focus and stigma associated with these programs were harmful to children, limited their referrals.

For the next 3 years (1996–1999), I followed events surrounding teachers' attempts to retain the narrative reporting system and the assessment process it represented. This was more than an isolated practice. Rather, teachers saw it as central to the inclusive curriculum and instructional practices at Betsy Miller. The narrative assessment also represented a significant manifestation of deeper levels of the school's culture. It engaged processes that reflected an integration of collegiality and compassionate caring into practice. Following teachers' attempts to maintain a practice built on values and beliefs that contradicted those of the larger education system would provide insight into issues surrounding the sustainability of progressive reforms in public schools.

Much of the literature demonstrating the power of school cultures to resist imposed change has focused on the difficulty of initiating and sustaining, within traditional public schools, reforms that reflect progressive, democratic, and learner-centered ideologies. Rather than transforming schools, progressive reforms themselves become transformed to fit the dominant culture (Sarason, 1996). The failure of the "mainstreaming" movement to provide an education for children with disabilities in the "least restrictive environment" is one example. Instead of adapting the school environment to the child, as intended by the "least restrictive environment" clause of the Individuals with Disabilities Act (1990), the burden of change was placed on the child, allowing the school system to maintain its value and belief in "ableness" as a criterion for belonging (Bogdan & Kugelmass, 1984; Kunc, 2000).

The challenges facing Betsy Miller stood this predicament on its head. This school's stated purpose was to provide educational programs built on acceptance and appreciation of *all* children during a time when the inclusion of students with special educational needs in general education classrooms was not the norm in its school district or state. Teachers' attempts to maintain the narrative assessment process demonstrate the limitations of analyses of school reform that neither considers the positionality of reforms and reformers nor the kinds of resistance possible within a hierarchical bureaucracy. Betsy Miller's position of relative powerlessness within larger systems and the absence of a strong, positional leader during a historical period when the agendas of state and federal governments stood in opposition to its culture limited teachers' ability to resist change. The sustainability of this school's norms and traditions were not as certain as those whose cultures reflected the dominant social order.

Teachers' resistance to the new report card reflected their awareness of the significance of assessment processes in maintaining an inclusive school. They believed comparing children to external standards rather than using each child's strengths, interests, individual development, and familial culture to establish annual goals was a "violation of our culture." This perception was so pervasive that some advocated a public presentation of resistance to the superintendent's directive. There was considerable support for that position among groups of professionals in the community, as well as among both middle-class and low-income minority parents. The parents I spoke with were particularly impressed with how well the narrative assessment process demonstrated teachers' knowledge and understanding of their children. Although the majority of parents at the school did not join in openly protesting the new report card, most believed the narrative assessment process should be retained.

A small group of parents, some of whom were also teachers at the school, organized public demonstrations and a sit-in at the superintendent's office to protest the imposition of the new report card. Bumper stickers were passed out, and one parent carried a sign saying, "Little boxes made of ticky-tacky and they all look the same—Our children are not boxes or the same." A letter-writing campaign to the local newspaper began. Some, like the following, commented on the relationship of the assessment process to the school's values and emphasized how the school district's behavior insulted teachers' professional integrity:

> The strength of this school has been in working as a school community to improve the school and develop its unique qualities.
>
> It is very disturbing that the new district administration seems not to recognize the harm that comes to the morale and pride of the school when there appears to be neither recognition nor respect for its efforts.

I am a parent of two children at [Betsy Miller]. I have great respect for the professional abilities of the teachers and staff, and I am
very aware of their anger and feelings of disempowerment over this
issue.

Although the letter-writing campaign reflected considerable support for
the narrative assessment process, there were parents who expressed concern
for its lack of clarity. They wanted to know where their child stood in relation to the academic performance of other students in the school district.

Collaborative Decision Making: The Site-Based Council

Teachers began to realize that open defiance of a superintendent's directive could be seen as insubordination, leading to dismissal or reassign-
ment. Calling on the skills they developed during the school's transformation, they asked parents to join them in formal negotiations with the school
district to resolve the conflict. A legitimate structure for these kinds of
negotiations, the Site-Based Council (SBC), had been established in 1993
under the previous State Department of Education administration to support shared decision making at schools. Betsy Miller's staff was, in fact,
the first in this school district to organize an effective SBC, applying other
experiences with collaborative processes to shared governance and decision
making with parents and other community participants. The model they
established would eventually be used in other schools throughout the district. The following description of the SBC is taken from the school's Web
site and illustrates how it reflected the larger school culture:

> The Betsy Miller Council is a diverse group of parents, staff, and com-
> munity members involved in decision making at our school. Decisions
> are made by consensus. The Council has developed the following
> working vision and mission statements:

OUR VISION FOR BETSY MILLER SCHOOL

> Betsy Miller Elementary School is a diverse and alive community that
> belongs to everybody and where everybody belongs. Each person is
> supported, nurtured, and safe to learn and grow.

MISSION OF THE SITE-BASED DECISION-MAKING COUNCIL

> To provide leadership which supports innovation, diversity, reflec-
> tion, and accountability for our children and their education. To cre-
> ate and maintain clear communication and accessible networks that
> involve everyone in the decisions that matter to them.

I attended SBC meetings from November 1996 through March 1997, observing teachers, parents, and members of the community collaborate to develop a plan that would keep the narrative assessment process in place. After their first meeting with the district's assistant superintendent in early November 1996, teachers recognized that more was at stake than the assessment process. Given the central school district's power to impose practices on their school, they needed to interact differently with central office administration than they did with one another. The following transcription from the November SBC meeting captures the understanding that they faced a "a clash of values" that required strategic thinking and behavior:

Teacher A: The assistant superintendent said we were very emotional and hysterical about this. He is very reactive.

Teacher B: We *are* passionate about this.

Teacher C: His remark is very sexist. We need to try to find out whose decision this really is.

Teacher B: I have heard that there is a waiver process that one of my colleagues told me about. I am going to check this out.

Teacher D: The staff is committed. We need to hear from the Council if they will support us.

Parent A: As a parent I want us to take it on.

To "take it on," teachers put personal differences aside to work with parents and the central administration through the SBC and eventually secured a waiver that exempted Betsy Miller from using the district's report card. The narrative assessment and reporting system would be maintained for 3 years, but alterations would be required. After making some changes to the system, a second waiver would be granted for another 3 years, to end in September 2003.

Compromise: Taking On and Taking Up the Dominant Culture

As teachers engaged in debates, strategized, and critiqued the narrative reporting system amongst themselves, their commitment to supporting student diversity through inclusion remained intact. Personal conflicts about how to achieve this, however, would begin to emerge. Although they tried to keep these conflicts hidden, tensions between individual teachers became evident at staff meetings, as well as the biweekly meetings of the SBC. These differences would not be visible at the two public meetings where a unified public face was presented to larger groups of parents, district administrators, and the general public when the new report card, general issues related to assessment, instruction, and newly imposed state standards were discussed and debated. It had become obvious to staff that their position of relative powerlessness in the school district required compromises both to their practice and how they expressed themselves publicly.

Rather than evidence of weakness or complicity, these compromises demonstrate what Munro (1998) describes as the conscious "taking up" of dominant beliefs to sustain commitments to more important concerns. Working with the school district allowed teachers to sustain a practice central to the school's inclusive culture, illustrating what Weiler (1988) describes as the "dialectical relationship between structural forces and consciousness or agency" (p. 102) needed to maintain autonomy when operating within a bureaucratic system. Two 3-year waivers would be granted, requiring modifications to the narrative reporting system, but allowing it to continue. Student achievement needed to be aligned with newly adopted statewide learning standards. To meet this new requirement, parents and teachers came together to develop rubrics and performance standards consistent with both state standards and the constructivist curriculum used at the school. Technical aspects of the reporting system were changed, but these alterations had minimal impact on the learner-centered, collaborative teaching and assessment processes central to the inclusive, classroom-based instructional practices that had evolved at Betsy Miller.

Some teachers and parents continued to believe that imposing performance standards and rubrics on the assessment process were inconsistent with teaching strategies built on children's strengths. Others saw performance standards as improving both the assessment process and instruction. Their concerns focused on the political and social realities facing the school and its children. Not acknowledging statewide standards could jeopardize the school and fail to prepare students to meet the expectations of the dominant culture. That, they argued, would violate the core value of the school, the "bottom line . . . a general view of children; that children come first." Without a person to mediate these disputes, disagreements between teachers would eventually widen, turning some teachers against others, and erode collegial relationships central to the school's culture.

SUSTAINING COLLEGIALITY THROUGH SHARED COMMITMENTS

From 1996–1999, commitments to inclusive values and a resolve to work with the school district were supported by teachers' relationships with one another. Individually, teachers did not have the power to resist imposed change, but working together they became effective negotiators. They had learned the importance of compromise in coming to consensus.

My constant presence at the school, during periods of both calm and crisis, provided numerous opportunities to observe these processes. Reaching consensus meant a decision would not be final until everyone agreed to live with the negotiated solution. Maintaining a collaborative school community required small compromises throughout the day. Teachers sought consensus with children around their choices of books, which activity to do first, where to sit and with whom to work. At goal-setting meetings, teachers negotiated with parents and children to establish a shared set of learning priorities. Differences among collaborators regarding how to work with specific children were similarly resolved.

Maintaining a dialectical relationship between autonomy and collaboration had become central to practices that reflected the staff's belief in the value of diversity and inclusion. In each of these instances, collective interests, values, and beliefs balanced individual needs, desires, and strengths. Consensus and compromise accommodated and supported autonomy. As in other situations, deeply felt differences among teachers were moderated by collaborative decision making, leading to consensus.

During his 7 years as principal, Joe developed strong personal relationships with staff, heightening his commitments and theirs. These relationships might even be described as symbiotic, with Joe and teachers depending on one another to sustain a school culture that fed their enthusiasm and, in turn, was sustained by their commitments. Traditional boundaries between the role of principal and teacher became blurred, with teachers having more authentic decision-making power than typically found in public schools. This relationship resembled what Lambert et al. (2002) describe as *constructivisit leadership*, that is, leadership that involved interactive process by students and teachers as well as the principal. Hierarchical structures within the school were replaced by shared responsibility in a community characterized by agreed values and hopes.

This kind of leadership is not unique to Betsy Miller and has been identified as central to collaborative and collegial relationships between teachers and positional leaders (i.e., principals) in schools with inclusive cultures (Kugelmass & Ainscow, 2003; Riehl, 2000; Udvari-Solnar & Keyes, 2000). Other investigations of successful leadership in schools that serve diverse populations of students have identified the structural components of this kind of distributed leadership (Spillane, Halverson, & Diamond, 2001), leadership behaviors (Udvari-Solnar & Keyes, 2000), cognitive processes (Maehr & Midgley, 1996), and affective and other personal characteristics of effective leaders (Carlson, 1996). The relationships established between Joe and teachers at Betsy Miller could be thought of as representing both transactional and transformational leadership. *Transac-*

tional leadership is based on the exchange of beliefs and motivations between formal leaders and followers for their mutual benefit. *Transformational leadership* includes this sharing of beliefs but also has a moral imperative: "Motivated by such deep values as freedom, community and justice, transformational leadership is not just concerned with what works but with what is good" (R. Evans, 1996, p. 168).

Although the moral dimension of transformational leadership was evident in Joe's commitment to educational equity and social justice, this concept does not fully explain how collaborative leadership evolved at Betsy Miller or was sustained. The emotional attachment that developed between Joe and Betsy Miller's teachers was as essential as their shared commitments. As Carlson (1996) points out, "Leaders in organizations must deal with basic human drives of love and aggression and with feelings and attitudes of dependency and control, conflict and compromise, and hostility and compassion" (p. 154). The significance of teachers' emotional life to what went on at Betsy Miller was constantly revealed in the ways they talked about each other and recalled past events. Even when they disagreed, their relationships motivated collective action that, at times, could have jeopardized their positions in the existing bureaucracy. The descriptions of their relationships reflected what Ferguson (cited in Carlson, 1996) refers to as "feminist discourse . . . a way of thinking and acting that is neither an extension of bureaucratic forms nor a mirror image of them" (p. 327).

From 1996–2000, four principals followed Joe, none lasting more than a year. The emotional impact of these shifts on teachers became apparent at a party I attended in August 1997 to celebrate the return to school the following week. Teachers from Betsy Miller had learned a few days earlier that the principal who had been with them for the past year had resigned. Only a little more than a year after Joe's death, her departure restimulated deeply held fears. During the following conversation at the party, two teachers and a parent member of the Site-Based Council discovered one another's nightmares.

Teacher A: I dreamed that I went to my classroom and instead of desks there were tombstones.
Parent A: I dreamed the school was a train and it had crashed.
Teacher B: I dreamed I came to school and the kids were running all over the place. It was chaos. I saw an adult from the back—I think it was the principal [who just resigned]. It was a woman who looked like her from the back. When I touched her shoulder to ask what was going on, she turned around and on her face was pasted this big, fake clown smile. It was very scary.

The lack of attention to emotional aspects of the relationships that existed between Betsy Miller's teachers and Joe would make it difficult for the principals that followed him to develop the kind of collegiality needed for the long-term sustainability of collaborative leadership. They needed to understand that it would take time to develop trust for one another. New relationships needed to emerge in which clearly delineated leadership structures and roles could develop that would allow teachers to share responsibility with a new principal (Kugelmass & Ainscow, 2003). Although the three African American and one White women principals who followed Joe shared his commitment to inclusion, concerns for equity, and collaborative leadership, their understandings of collaboration were built on theoretical models that did not conform to what teachers at Betsy Miller had come to expect. During Joe's administration teachers became used to having an authentic voice and had little patience for any kind of hierarchical decision making. Unwilling and, at times, unable to conform to teachers' demands, each subsequent principal left Betsy Miller, taking positions in other schools. As one principal put it, "Those teachers were unsupervisable."

The lack of a consistent person in a leadership position from 1996–2000 did not, as it had in 1983–1987, lead to chaos or the immediate demise of the school's culture. Shared leadership systems had emerged among teachers that continued to be supported by shared values and beliefs. This allowed the school to continue during these 4 years much as it had during Joe's tenure. During that period, teachers worked to secure two waivers from the school district, allowing them to keep the narrative assessment process until 2003. Most remained sensitive to one another's needs and desires. Teachers had learned to interact with one another in ways that accommodated differences while maintaining commitments to core values and beliefs. Within this kind of collegial community, an informal collaborative and decentralized form of leadership evolved that sustained Betsy Miller's culture for the next few years.

Initially, I believed teachers' ability to secure the waiver and keep the narrative assessment process to be a symbolic indicator of their ability to sustain their school's culture in the absence of a consistent principal. I would soon discover it merely represented winning one battle. Sustaining other practices and maintaining the collegiality and caring central to the school's culture would require teachers' willingness to continue to engage in a collaborative, strategically designed, and prolonged struggle. Instead, a siege mentality began to develop, interfering with the ability to establish a collaborative partnership with each new principal that followed Joe. Collective management of the sometimes-contradictory demands from within and without the school required trusting relationships as well as political understanding, negotiation skills, and shared commitments.

Teachers needed to understand that school district governance structures required principals to take on certain roles and responsibilities. Joe had done this in ways that protected them from the external bureaucracy. In spite of what went on every day inside the school, he was still held accountable by a centralized, external management system for the performance of staff and students. He was, however, uniquely able to manipulate the system. Accepting and supporting a new person as their principal would require teachers to put aside the loss they felt after Joe's death and allow for the development of a new relationship. Quakie Onaygo described Joe as able to manage external demands in ways that were not possible for newer principals. A more bureaucratic climate in the district, state, and nation had created demands she believed would have even challenged his skills. By 2002 the context in which she and her colleagues were operating was tightening its hold on decision making by individual schools. She worried that some teachers and principals at Betsy Miller might use this new climate as an excuse to exclude low-income African American children from Betsy Miller.

> We've inherited people [administrators] that are "to the book." And when you are "to the book" and implementing "to the book" it's always going to have a disparate impact on a population. So, for example, we always had kids in this building who shouldn't have gotten on the bus because technically they were open-enrolled students [i.e., students not living in the neighborhoods designated for attendance at Betsy Miller]. But *we* knew this was the place they were supposed to be. So we always figured out how to wiggle around that so that kid could get on the bus. Now that we're implementing the open-enrollment policy to the letter, which was of course always a very classist policy only available to a certain population and profile of kids [i.e., parents have to drive kids to school if they are not from the designated neighborhood], it has had a disparate impact for our young kids from downtown. So, just because of that decision, as one of many, we have lost seven African American males, all kids who seemed to spend more time in the office then they needed to. They are out on a technicality that this isn't their home school, but really no one wanted them here.

She saw little, if any, objection from teachers to using the open-enrollment policy to remove these children from the school. She believed this decision reflected a loss of a shared commitment to diversity and inclusion.

Quakie returned to Betsy Miller in 2002 after several years as a middle school teacher and administrator. She wanted to "return home" before retiring. Her perception of what had changed there since she left in 1989 provided insights into the ways in which primary-level commitments that had supported collegiality at Betsy Miller were beginning to erode. She offered her perspective on which things at the school were the same and which were different:

> One of the things that I think is the same is that you hear the termi-nology around multiculturalism and diversity and difference. The lan-guage is still very much there; I'm not sure the practice is much there. There is also a clear absence of teachers of color. That was not the case when I was here [in 1989]. That's not the case with paraprofes-sional staff who are largely people of color. But the imbalance, I'm afraid, conveys some unspoken messages to our kids, and so largely the decisions that are being made about children are by people who don't look like them and unfortunately—depending on when they were hired—a good many of them have been hired since Joe. So, they don't remember what we were here for. And we are presently, I think, working without a mission. We are not working as a total building, on the same page. We have individual teachers who have a vision for where they see their kids going, but schoolwide it doesn't exist.
>
> I think it's very sad because it couldn't get any better here than where it was for kids. I'm afraid it's turning a little bit more into a building that is not terribly different from other buildings; where deci-sions are made largely in the interest of adults and not in the [interest of] children. And we have become so skilled at using language that sounds appropriate at Betsy Miller, but it doesn't get translated in our work with kids. We are suspending more African American males then any other population. I think that it's statistically relevant [that] we still have a disproportionate number of kids on Title I roles, and even more serious, African American males are being labeled emotion-ally disturbed. This is something that was unheard of in the old Betsy Miller.
>
> I just thought [coming back to Betsy Miller] was going to be so great. There were people I had enormous respect for and I knew re-spected me. People who were committed to keeping the kid in front of them at all times. That was the one thing Joe always forced us to ask ourselves: "At the end of the day, the decisions you make about other people's children, were they truly in the interest of the child?"
>
> I also don't see faculty meeting agendas focusing on kid issues. I

don't see grade-level meetings focusing on how to meet the needs of a population of kids that we have clearly identified as not making it. We seem to be much more focused on busywork. You know, things that take an awful lot of time to do. I know that paperwork is only going to go someplace and sit. And we put all this time on reflecting on our social studies objectives for the year, and there seems to be this panic that this is done right away. That stuff isn't going to get us anywhere. In the meantime, in all of our rooms this year are kids with some serious issues and we're not using our experience and insights. And we have an enormously talented staff on this floor. And [the fourth-and-fifth-grade team], we're the most experienced in this building. We're the oldest—the geriatric ward—the long-termers who were here from the beginning who ought to know better.

I think we have moved away from our mission. There is no mission. We are all kinda doing our own thing, based on our individual philosophies. We are not moving as a whole staff around anything. We've lost the vision. It feels so much more for me like the other schools. We're putting much more energy into making decisions that work for adults and not so much for kids. For example, I worked with Joe in three different buildings, and we always ate with kids in our classrooms. Such an important time to build a sense of community by breaking bread together. It's that time to get that one-on-one with that particular kid that you knew missed something that morning. Just the whole eating together cements the family-feel of the classroom. Now there are some teachers who are going by the contract, which is something we never did in this building in the past. Contractually, classroom teachers are entitled to so much time and lunch hour. So, they're wanting that now. They want the kids to eat in the lunchroom. This is a terrible decision for kids. So much will happen around that. It will probably be in place next year [i.e., fall 2003].

The principal at Betsy Miller from 2000–2002 offered a different perspective than Quakie on the stricter enforcement of open-enrollment policies and teacher commitments. This local African American woman, Marilyn Barker, came out of retirement at the request of the superintendent after the fourth principal left. She supported the school's vision of inclusion and was instrumental in securing the second 3-year waiver for the narrative reporting system. Unlike Quakie, she believed teachers' rigid allegiance to past practices and resistance to change would be their ultimate downfall. Focusing on the changing context in which schools are now operating, Marilyn emphasized the need for teachers to accommodate new demands. This included their need to rethink curriculum and include instructional practices, such as direct instruction, that she believed might better serve some low-income, minority children.

She did not see the tightening of the open-enrollment policy as reflecting the loss of the school's culture but rather its success. Its popularity among middle-class African American and White families had come about because of its reputation as an inclusive school. Parents of children with high levels of special educational needs that were the consequence of autism and other significant learning disabilities wanted their children to attend Betsy Miller. The school's experience including these children in general education classrooms and its collaborative teaching and teaming attracted these parents. The increased interest in Betsy Miller was, however, taking place during a time when budget deficits limited the number of specialists the school district was able to provide to support and accommodate children with special needs. Betsy Miller was now competing with other schools for these services. Unlike 10 years earlier, it was not the only inclusive school in the district. Only two elementary schools still maintained self-contained special education classrooms. The others were demanding the same level of support in classrooms from related service providers, special education, reading, and ESL teachers that were once unique to Betsy Miller.

Quakie and Marilyn did agree that regardless of their motivation, by 2002 the teachers at Betsy Miller were exhausted by the demands they continued to face. Some responded by retreating to their own classrooms, attending only required team meetings; others would retire. Some, like Karen Shriver, who once said, "I couldn't teach anywhere else," transferred to other schools. Karen related her leaving to the lack of leadership she believed was needed by teachers in order to accommodate the new demands they faced:

> Some of us were more involved with looking at some of the state standards and having a commitment to our kids doing well on the tests. We felt that we needed to change our school because the outside world was very different. We no longer had the luxury that we weren't going to be taking some standardized tests, and that wasn't going to impact the kind of teaching [we did]. And so, when that started happening and there was no leadership, and people were holding on to what they believe, it felt like a division between those who really held on to a really strong developmental approach and those who really were concerned about some direct teaching so children could be successful on some of the tests they needed to take. And the total lack of leadership that was needed to really help us through that—I think we could have done it [with leadership].

In the early years of the school's development, Karen was one of the teachers who championed a developmental approach for all children at Betsy Miller. She had been instrumental in moving Belinda and other African American teachers to accept whole-language instruction. These colleagues, however, also influenced her teaching, as had parents and the students she worked with over the years. The changing reality of public education that now included high-stakes tests for all children had also moved Karen to recognize the need for instructional compromise that included preparing students for these tests. This would be seen as treason by some colleagues. Karen described how the conflicts that began to emerge around these issues and the breakdown of decision-making processes contributed to her decision to leave the school in 2002.

> We continued to have team meetings . . . the structure stayed completely the same, but no decisions were ever made. Everybody was allowed to have a voice. We believed everything was going to be consensus but nothing ever happened because of course you could never get consensus. And so I felt like we just kept mulling over and mulling over and mulling over and we never moved. [I'm one of those] people who needed to see some steps moved forward. We just kept having these huge discussions about the same thing.

SUSTAINING COMPASSIONATE CARE

Schools are more than buildings where principals and teachers work and children study. They are places where staff, children, and parents develop important relationships with one another. At Betsy Miller, these relationships were built over time and rested on a shared commitment to compassionate caring for one another and for children. Although most of the teachers I spoke with believed this commitment had not diminished substantially, they recognized that changing demands required the development of a different definition of what was in children's best interests. It will be difficult to sustain the school's culture for more than a few more years without leadership that can bring teachers together to reach consensus on what they believe is best for kids.

Pat Carini (2001) might have been thinking of Joe Stefano when she wrote the following:

> I think about administrators I have known who understood their work, and especially the work of leadership, to pivot on *caring for* the intellectual and social life of the school. Administrators, that is, who steal time from the paperwork and other bureaucratic tasks they are paid to do in order to frame issues

so they are talkable, in order to make collaborative work and study opportunities for teachers, in order to bring parents and others in the community into the school, in order to create *public spaces* for shared perspectives. (p. 114)

Karen's decision to leave Betsy Miller would ultimately be influenced by the loss of these kinds of spaces and the deterioration of her relationships with colleagues. She felt their trust and respect diminish as she argued against practices she believed were no longer in the best interest of children. Personal relationships that had been central to collaboration were being undermined by ideologically based differences that provided no room for compromise. Some teachers perceived Karen's changing position in support of direct instruction for some children as an invalid portrayal of caring for children. Karen describes her changing position this way:

No matter what you do, you have to change. And I felt like Betsy Miller was no longer changing with any direction. They were changing just by becoming slack and not really following through. That's my perception of what was happening. And I just felt really strongly that I suddenly was not giving children what they needed there because what they needed was suddenly very different. Because of the standards and all of that. And I became really frustrated.

So it just started feeling real personal and I didn't feel good as a teacher, and I could cry about it now because, you know, kids' needs weren't met. So that was really hard. . . . And I said, "You know what? Life is too short to feel this stress."

Before speaking with Karen, I hadn't considered that *sustaining change* was an oxymoron. As she explained, "No matter what you do, you have to change." Her decision to leave was not a consequence of any one specific change in practice or structure. The blended services model was still in place, and teachers continued to collaborate with one another. Deeper levels of the school's culture, however, were beginning to erode. Most important was the lack of agreement about what represented compassionate care for children. Karen knew that Betsy Miller would never look like the school she had helped create from 1987–1995, nor would it become the same dysfunctional environment the staff had inherited. Those earlier incarnations reflected responses to different social contexts. To sustain the school's culture now required responding to new external realities while remaining true to its underlying values and beliefs. Without strong leadership this seemed impossible to Karen.

By 2003 the waiver allowing the narrative assessment process to be used in place of the district report card will expire, and Betsy Miller's teachers will find themselves working within an even more hierarchical system than when the waiver was granted. Sustaining the narrative assessment process for 6 years, without a principal as their leader, demonstrated that they had developed strong collaborative problem-solving and conflict-resolution skills, and an understanding and appreciation of the expertise of others. In spite of this, they will not be able to sustain their school's culture in the current political climate without maintaining strong trusting relationships with one another and a principal who shares their commitments. Without collegiality and shared commitments, teachers' ability to sustain their school's culture is uncertain.

SUSTAINING A COMMUNITY OF PRACTICE

Investigations of schools with sustained commitments to particular beliefs and values demonstrate that neither specific practices nor particular organizational structures account for their sustainability. Rather, it is a school's capacity to sustain its "organizational identity" in the community, in spite of surface change, that appears to support cultural continuity (Herbert & Hatch, 2001).

> In the long term, schools should be able to adapt to changes in their environments without *completely* [emphasis mine] altering the basic philosophies and ideologies that have always informed their practices. An organizational identity, which guides what is important, what is appropriate, and what is effective, is a broad framework that provides flexibility for adaptation and change, while constraining choices so that practices and goals remain *relatively* [emphasis mine] consistent. (p. 22)

Betsy Miller has continued to maintain its identity in its community as the school most responsive to and supportive of student diversity. It has become the school of choice for many nontraditional families as well as for parents whose children have been identified as having special educational needs. It has, however, shifted from its earlier focus on racial and socioeconomic equity to more diffuse commitments. Sandy Walden described this shift:

> I think you know that clustering children of like background is still maintained at Betsy Miller [in 2003]. We typically cluster African American kids, kids from gay, bisexual, or lesbian families, and ESL children [in the same classrooms]. Some parents request that we not

use these criteria to place their children, and we generally listen. We now have a program here called COLAGE for children of lesbians and gays, that the kids can participate in with parental permission first. ESL kids get additional instruction and some other special programming. I don't know of anything specific that happens for African American kids, except that many teachers try to maintain an Afrocentric focus wherever possible.

Maybe we're all just overwhelmed by the new state standards, because the exciting latest things at Betsy Miller are so often about interesting academic issues, math, comprehension, special ed, or even about social issues such as antiviolence programs. Their underpinnings consider culture, background, but basically I'm thinking that so much of what happened in those years for those of us who have been teaching here for a long time has been internalized. We treat children with the utmost of respect; we consider their culture and individuality; and we try to compose a curriculum that is appropriate, exciting, engaging. . . . Much of this has been transmitted to the staff that came on board close to Joe's departure, but I'm not sure all the new teachers get it.

By 2002 the majority of teachers remaining at Betsy Miller had not participated in its earlier transformation. Most never knew Joe Stefano, and some new teachers even resented his name being used as the justification for instructional practices and schoolwide structures. They were attracted to teaching at Betsy Miller because of its continuing reputation as a school committed to diversity and inclusion, but had little, if any, emotional attachment to maintaining structures and practices developed before they were hired. They wanted to be part of a "community of practice" (Wenger, 1998) in which teachers' understanding of inclusion was sustained by their work with children and interactions with one another. Holding on to practices that no longer reflected the reality of the context they found themselves working within might, in fact, interfere with sustaining the kind of collaboration and collegiality central to inclusive schools. New teachers' voices needed to be included in the changing reality of day-to-day life, while remaining true to the values and beliefs that were the foundation of the school's culture. Sustaining a culture of inclusion required the continuation of a context in which teachers' "situated knowledge" (Lave & Wenger, 1991) was embedded in an interconnected network compassionate care.

CHAPTER 7

Implications for Creating and Sustaining Inclusive Schools

One might argue that Betsy Miller's story is too idiosyncratic to be of much use to others in very different contexts. Located in a university town set in the midst of a pristine rural county in the northeastern United States, the school is somewhat atypical. The community it serves is privileged in having many educational and cultural resources. My intention in telling its story is not, however, to present a cultural description that relates only to this specific place. Rather, the story of this one school demonstrates the significance and limitations of teacher empowerment in creating and sustaining inclusive school cultures. Those committed to promoting social justice through their work as teachers are particularly vulnerable during periods when demands for accountability conflict with maintaining the values and beliefs that lie at the heart of these kinds of schools.

As in all interpretive ethnographies, a good deal more emerged than the story of one school's evolution. Some of what was learned was the consequence of unexpected tragedies, Joe Stephano's death in 1996 being the most obvious. Grief engulfed the school like a heavy fog, shrouding every classroom door. Guided by concern for children, teachers allowed in as much as they believed their students could manage. Only when they left their rooms to meet with one another, did teachers express the depth of their loss. After the immediate shock of Joe's passing, some became mobilized by his memory to work toward obtaining the waiver from the school district that allowed for the continuation of the narrative assessment process until 2003. For others, the emotional impact of his passing would interfere with maintaining and establishing collegial relationships with old and new colleagues. The September 11 (2001) tragedy would further dampen motivation for change, fueling fears and heightening some teachers' reluctance to challenge the status quo. The world was becoming too uncertain a place to consider more than getting through each day.

These and other events described in previous chapters may have been unique to this specific time and place, but are not very different from the challenges every teacher faces. Some are personal and close to home, others more global. In each circumstance, what goes on outside classrooms affects teachers personally and shapes their interactions with colleagues, children, and parents. This has been true for teachers in every generation, but has the greatest impact on those who see their role as including the promotion of social justice. Betsy Miller's story provides an example of how one such group of teachers were called upon to face unanticipated events that impacted on their lives and work at a time when their school confronted significant challenges to its inclusive culture. Their responses have important implications for creating and sustaining inclusive schools elsewhere.

This concluding chapter examines the broader implications of what happened at Betsy Miller for the preparation of new teachers, provision of ongoing support for practicing teachers, and the nature of leadership in inclusive schools. This examination highlights the importance of preparing and supporting teachers to face the unexpected and unanticipated events that characterize life in schools. Leadership in inclusive schools is then examined and redefined through a comparative analysis of leadership at Betsy Miller with that found at inclusive schools in the United Kingdom whose cultures support collaborative structures and instructional practices. Their shared commitments to compassionate care placed children at the center of educational decision making. These cultural commitments will be shown as central to the kind of leadership needed for promoting and sustaining progressive school reform.

IMPLICATIONS FOR TEACHER PREPARATION AND DEVELOPMENT

In many regions of the United States, schools remain segregated by race and social class, in spite of federal and state civil rights legislation. The racial and sociocultural integration seen in some school districts does not, however, indicate that educational inequities have been eliminated in those places. Rather, in schools with diverse student populations, poor educational performance is greater among children from low-income and non-White families than among more affluent and dominant-culture students. Within these schools, poor and minority-culture children are also overrepresented among those classified for special education and placed in separate special education classrooms. In December 1998, for example, the federal education department's civil rights division, for the second time in 2 years, cited New York City for "inordinately large numbers of Black and Latino students [in] special-education classes, which often become holding pens for children who learn nothing and rarely graduate" ("A Special-Ed Warning," 1998, p. 26A).

A similar situation exists in the region where Betsy Miller is located. In 1999 this region was among those with the highest rate of segregated programs for children identified for special education in its state and had disproportionate numbers of students from low-income and minority families in self-contained special education classrooms. In this context Betsy Miller was again unique. A 2-year investigation by the United States Department of Education ("A Special-Ed Warning," 1998), found that the highest rates of placements of African American children in special education classrooms occurred in schools where the principal, faculty, and other children were mostly White. The study concluded that teachers' lack of time or skills and ethnic stereotyping combined with structural incentives to remove children from the mainstream. Placement in special education classes removed the problem child from the classroom, but it neither resolved his or her educational problems nor forced general educators to examine their own practices. Consequently, the values, beliefs, and assumptions underlying the system remained unchallenged, perpetuating the inequalities that characterize public education.

At Betsy Miller, not only was every child included in general education classrooms, but also every aspect of its culture supported what Ladson-Billings (1994) identifies as "culturally relevant pedagogy." These practices evolved in a school where the majority of teachers had always been White women. Only during the first 3 years of Joe Stephano's tenure as principal was there what one African American teacher called a "healthy number" of African American teachers. Those five teachers exerted considerable influence within their instructional teams. Through their relationships with White colleagues, these African American teachers urged and supported the development of skills teachers needed to serve a diverse student population. As Quakie Onaygo recalled, this required every teacher, Black and White, to examine his or her internalized assumptions about children, parents, and colleagues.

> It was a painful process, a lot of tears because people had to face their racism; they had to face their classism; they had to face their homophobia; they had to face all that stuff that we didn't even really know that we carried around with us but had a huge impact on our practice with kids. And so it was a fascinating time to work with a population of people who breathed and thought and felt the same way and had the same outcomes for all kids. It was my only experience with it. It was magical and very, very rare. I have never been a part of anything like it before and haven't since.

An ESL teacher who recently retired from Betsy Miller believes the strong commitments to racial equity that characterized this "magical" period diminished as each African American teacher left the school. By 2002 Quakie would be the only African American teacher remaining.

The lack of diversity among the teaching staff at Betsy Miller is similar to that found in most public schools in the United States, where the majority of elementary school teachers are White, middle-class women (Johnson, 2002). The same is true among students in most teacher education programs, in spite of active recruiting of students of color (Wideen, Mayer-Smith, & Moon, 1998). Although it is important to consider how the absence of teachers of color helps create and sustain school cultures built on values and beliefs that stigmatize some children, their absence cannot be used as an excuse for not elevating teachers' understanding of the ways their internalized beliefs impact on their ability to successfully educate all children. Quakie's insights point out that whether or not they resemble their students, all teachers need to examine the deeply seated and often unconscious assumptions they bring to their work. These kinds of teachers formed the "critical mass" essential to creating the tipping point for change at Betsy Miller.

The experiences of teachers at Betsy Miller now informs my work in preparing mostly White female students to become elementary and special education teachers. The graduate students with whom I work are excited about the possibility of becoming teachers who create classrooms in schools that respond positively to student diversity. They are not wedded to any one instructional method, but rather to adapting curriculum and instruction to fit the learning and behavioral styles, cultures, and experiences of children. These new teachers understand that the successful inclusion of children with disabilities and other special educational needs, non-English speakers, and other minorities, will require calling upon a wide repertoire of instructional strategies that includes both behavioral and constructivist practices adapted to the abilities, needs, interests, cultures, and experiences of specific children. These adaptations may include direct instruction in specific skills, scaffolded assistance using strategic learning approaches, and behavior modification or adjustments to the physical environment, as well as providing an enriched and culturally relevant content. They also understand that the appropriateness of the content and process of instruction needs to be determined by what they know about a child. The instructional goals they establish will be guided by information gathered through systematic observations of children and children's work and developed in collaboration with parents, colleagues, and children (Rainforth & Kugelmass, 2003).

The experience of Betsy Miller's teachers demonstrates the importance of encouraging teachers to reflect on the influence of internalized assumptions and dominant educational paradigms on their work. Principles of feminist pedagogy are particularly relevant to this aspect of teacher preparation as well as for the continuing education of practicing teachers. Initially designed to empower women to challenge the status quo and trust their own insights, feminist teaching encourages teachers to make connections between their own experiences and the issues they confront in their schools and classrooms. Acting as critical friends working in pairs or on teams, teachers are asked to examine their own assumptions and support one another, making connections between experiences, feelings, and the content of their learning. Through this process teachers not only gain confidence "in thinking for themselves, in listening to their inner voices, in speaking up" (Sleeter & Grant, 1999, p. 137) but also experience the kinds of supportive relationships central to inclusive school cultures.

These processes are particularly important for teachers whose cultural background and personal experiences differ dramatically from their students. Reflecting on their own experiences as children in public schools and in school-based field placements can lead teachers to confront contradictions between what they have been told are best practices and the reality of public education. Once they leave the supportive academic environment of their teacher education programs, these new teachers will continually need to reconcile bureaucratic demands, as well as those from other teachers, administrators, and parents, with what they believe is best for children. To do this, they need more than a wide and flexible repertoire of instructional strategies. As was true for the teachers at Betsy Miller, being instrumental in creating inclusive schools will also require knowing how to face dilemmas, solve problems, and resolve conflicts.

Action research and other types of projects directed at solving real-life problems that may be obstacles to the creation of inclusive schools can be effective for linking theory with practice, building teachers' confidence, and developing the courage to embrace the lifelong task of creative problem resolution when multiple courses of action are possible, and no conclusively correct answers exist (Wideen, Mayer-Smith & Moon, 1998). Integrating these kinds of activities into teacher education helps teachers understand how the structures that guide and shape public education support their own resistance to the pedagogical and structural changes needed to connect education to the lived experiences of children. When teachers do these activities as collaborative projects in work groups, they also explore group processes, further enabling the development of the skills and dispositions they will need as collaborators in inclusive schools while enhancing their capacity for reflexivity and flexibility.

Although new and experienced teachers respond favorably when course content is connected to their experiences in schools, most continue to approach problem solving from a positivist point of view. Betsy Miller's teachers developed strategies and structures for problem solving and problem resolution built on an understanding that most of the issues they faced would never be fully resolved. Whether developing curriculum, working with children and families, negotiating school systems, or interacting with colleagues, they saw themselves as always "in process." These teachers recognized how a shared belief system, supported by caring for one another, was essential for living and working with irresolvable dilemmas. Unlike these teachers, many of my students have not yet developed an understanding of the recursive nature of the problem-solving process. They look for absolute and permanent solutions for conflicts with children, parents, other teachers, and administrators.

Although useful for raising consciousness and promoting reflection, action research projects, written journals, and classroom discussions are by themselves inadequate for moving many teachers toward accepting that there may never be an absolute resolution for some dilemmas. I have found that shifting the perception of problem solving from a linear to a recursive process requires the exploration of nonrational elements of experience. To do this, I include autobiographical storytelling, personal myth making, and visual imagery to help new and practicing teachers become aware of the ways in which curriculum and instruction reflect values, beliefs, and ideologies that can support or interfere with children's learning (see Kugelmass, 2000). These activities expand teachers' creativity and imagination and are adaptations of the work of others who acknowledge the significance of personal transformation in the preparation of teachers (Connelly & Clandinin, 1988; Greene, 1995; Regenspan, 2002; Witherell & Noddings, 1991).

The exercises I present to my students represent an application of Jungian theory (Laszlo, 1958), emphasizing the necessity of engaging the unconscious and nonrational processes in personal transformation and development. Jung demonstrated the ways in which a "personal unconscious" (Jung, 1951/1958), embedded within a "collective unconscious," develops through one's life experiences. Unexamined cultural and individual assumptions interfere with teachers' ability to negotiate life's obstacles. Resolution of personal dilemmas therefore requires the integration of precognitive elements of consciousness with cognitive processes. Generally not accessible through rational discourse, these elements can be brought to consciousness through teachers examination of the stories they tell themselves about schools, the personal myths they carry with them, and the symbols they use to represent each.

Becoming a teacher requires more than acquiring a body of knowledge or set of skills. It is a complex socialization process, analogous to a rite of passage. As in an aboriginal walkabout, a new teacher is sent into the wilderness, equipped with a few basic tools, knowledge gained from elders, and a spiritual system to assist with the emotional experience of the adventure. If successful, she emerges ready to assume a meaningful role in the community. In traditional preparation programs, new teachers are given knowledge and skills as tools to enter the profession and then are sent on their way. Although the cultural foundations for these tools may be acknowledged and critiqued in course work, new teachers' spiritual orientation remains grounded in belief systems embedded in the larger culture. This is particularly the case among those whose social, cultural, and economic background reflects the dominant culture. Their unspoken values and beliefs are generally consistent with the assumptions of dominant educational paradigms and rarely include an examination of the importance of compassionate care in education.

Programs designed to prepare activist teachers to adapt social-constructivist practices within a framework that includes a critical analysis of schooling similarly neglect the inner life of teachers. The new teachers who leave these programs have an even more perilous journey than those whose preparation programs embraced traditional views. Reform-minded teachers may be equipped with tools that include a wide repertoire of instructional strategies and a knowledge base that includes culturally relevant pedagogy, but the belief system providing the foundation for the "community of practice" (Wenger, 1998) that they are about to enter will often contradict the messages of their activist professors. To effect change in these kinds of settings, these new teachers need to be equipped with both an internalized belief system that supports the tools they bring with them and the emotional and spiritual resources necessary for survival in what will be a sometimes hostile land.

When I first read *The Hero with a Thousand Faces* (Campbell, 1949), I found the relationship of the following story to becoming a new teacher stunning. The journey into the unknown and subsequent defeat of the monster by a young prince who had just completed military training under a world-renowned teacher is offered as a metaphor for many life passages, including the entering of a new profession by a young person. Because he has become master in the use of five weapons, the prince in the story has been given the name Prince Five-Weapons. He sets out on a journey and eventually comes to a forest inhabited by an ogre, Sticky-Hair. Rather than avoiding the forest, the prince enters and confronts the monster. However, the ogre captures each of the five weapons in his sticky-hair. He then grabs the prince and is about to eat him, but stops, puzzled by the prince's lack of fear. When asked why he is not afraid, the prince replies, "Ogre, why should I be afraid? For in one life one death is absolutely certain. What's more, I have in my belly a thunderbolt for a weapon. If you eat me, you will not be able to digest that weapon. It will tear your insides to tatters and fragments and will kill you. In that case we'll both perish. That's why I'm not afraid" (p. 87).

Joseph Campbell offered the story to represent the limitations of our five senses (five weapons) in the face of seemingly insurmountable obstacles. "The passage of the mythological hero may be overground, incidentally; fundamentally it is inward—into depths where obscure resistances are overcome, and long lost, forgotten powers are revivified, to be made available for the transfiguration of the world" (p. 29). Parallels between Prince Five-Weapons and the experience of new teachers may seem somewhat tenuous. I have, however, come to understand the experience of working with challenging children in less than supportive contexts as a heroic journey for new and experienced teachers. In spite of the theoretical knowledge and instructional tools (five weapons) they bring with them from their preparation programs, many are fearful of trying approaches that seem different from those of other teachers or that challenge preexisting assumptions that provide the foundation for traditional educational practice.

Success in dealing with multiple demands and reconciling what appear to be incompatible perspectives among educators requires an unyielding commitment to children. These teachers must operate out of a fierce belief in compassionate care, analogous to the sixth weapon of the prince. Acknowledging and addressing the nonrational elements of the teaching-learning experience can assist new and experienced teachers to develop this "internal thunderbolt" and help them become teacher-warriors. Preparing teachers to work in equitable ways within inequitable educational systems requires new teachers who believe in their power to effect change. This calls for more than pedagogical knowledge and skills, social-political expertise, and a commitment to educational equity. An internalized sense of agency is also needed to resist dominant ideologies while conforming to institutional demands and, simultaneously, providing effective instruction for children (Casey, 1993; Kreisberg, 1992; Munro, 1998). Feminist scholars illustrate the ways in which empowered teachers, like those at Betsy Miller, can alter relationships with institutional bureaucracies to help achieve structural and pedagogical change within educational institutions (Antler & Biklen, 1990; Casey, 1993; Maehr & Midgley, 1996; Maeroff, 1988; Miller, 1990; Munro, 1998; Weiler, 1988). This requires the exploration of conscious and unconscious influences on practice and personal resistance to change.

The stories told by individual teachers at Betsy Miller illustrate that although personal empowerment is essential for understanding the way externally imposed assumptions and beliefs limit the willingness to take risks, it is not sufficient for creating and sustaining inclusive school cultures. There was no one hero responsible for this school's transformation. Rather it required a collective commitment to a shared vision by individually empowered individuals. These shared commitments were maintained through the relationships teachers established with one another, their principal, parents, and students. Important decisions were made collectively and, at times, required compromises that balanced individual with collective needs, desires, and concerns. These kinds of collaborative relationships reflect feminist beliefs in the importance of the connections individuals establish with others in defining and shaping moral judgment and action (Belenky et al., 1986; Evans, 1995; Gilligan, 1982).

IMPLICATIONS FOR LEADERSHIP IN INCLUSIVE SCHOOLS

The decision to expand the study of Karen Shriver's classroom into an investigation of the sustainability of the school's inclusive culture was prompted by Joe Stephano's transfer to another school. I was familiar with the importance of strong leadership in sustaining a school's culture. I also knew that reliance on a charismatic individual could leave an organization vulnerable once that person left. Given Betsy Miller's reputation as a maverick school and Joe's heroic image in the community as the person responsible for its development, I wondered what would happen here. Suzanne Millman was the first to point out how this concern reflected my internalization of the myth of Joe as heroic leader.

> Do you know the old feminist riddle about the father and son who were in a serious car accident? They are taken to the emergency room in a nearby hospital but when they get there, they are told they have to go to another hospital. This hospital didn't allow doctors to treat their own children. . . . I was an older student in a junior-level psychology class in college in 1971. Fifteen young women and myself were asked to figure out why they had to go to another hospital. None of us could figure it out. Our professor, who was also a woman, wanted to make the point about how set our thinking was in sexist stereotypes. We could not see that his *mother* [emphasis mine] was the emergency room doctor.

Just as her classmates were unable to see the boy's mother as the doctor, I was initially unaware of the significance of teacher leadership in creating and sustaining this school's inclusive culture. I would, however, eventually discover that leadership at Betsy Miller was not the jurisdiction of any one individual but rather distributed among the entire staff.

Investigations of leadership in inclusive schools that share Betsy Miller's collaborative and collegial dimensions and a commitment to supporting diversity among students have focused on the behavior and attitudes of principals. Riehl's (2000) study of principals of successful inclusive schools revealed individuals who, like Joe, fostered change through their "relentless commitment" to social justice and ideological belief in inclusion. These transformational leaders (Ingram, 1977) motivated staff by appealing to intrinsic desires rather than relying on extrinsic rewards. Teachers described these principals as people who inspire rather than coerce (Ingram, 1997).

Bailey and du Plessis (1997) surveyed 200 school principals and found that attitudes and commitments toward inclusion were a significant predictor of the quality of inclusive practice at their respective schools. Guzman (1997) identified several factors shared by principals in six successful inclusive schools that were also evident in Joe's work at Betsy Miller. All of these principals did the following things: (1) Establish systems of communication that provided opportunities for staff members to voice concerns and make recommendations for change; (2) become personally involved in dialogue with parents; (3) work collaboratively with staff to establish a shared philosophy of inclusion; (4) establish policies related to discipline issues with students; and (5) demonstrate effective problem-solving skills.

Although teachers are central to creating and sustaining a school's culture, a deep ideological commitment to inclusion by the person holding positional leadership as principal is clearly important for supporting a culture of inclusion. Identifying effective leadership behaviors for these individuals can help prepare principals to become effective managers of inclusive schools within bureaucratic school systems. This understanding is not sufficient, however, for understanding how inclusive schools work or for sustaining a school's inclusive culture when a transformational leader no longer holds a formal leadership position. It also renders teacher-leadership invisible, reinforcing the hegemonic belief in authoritarian leadership dominating American public education.

A Comparative Study of Leadership in Inclusive Schools

To expand my understanding of how leadership operates in inclusive schools, I turned to schools outside the United States (Kugelmass & Ainscow, 2003). In the fall of 2002, with support from the National College for School Leadership in the United Kingdom and working in collaboration with colleagues from the University of Manchester, I examined features of leadership at inclusive schools whose cultural dimensions closely matched Betsy Miller's. Two schools were selected for a comparative analysis of leadership. At each of these schools, children with disabilities and other special educational needs were placed in general education classrooms alongside culturally and linguistically diverse peers. Although operating within very different external contexts, their organizational structures and stated missions reflected the broadened definition of inclusive education found at Betsy Miller.

The cultures of these schools were examined by reviewing documents, reading previously complied case studies, observing in classrooms, and interviewing teachers and administrators. This examination did not have the depth of the full ethnographic examination carried out at Betsy Miller, but focused on understanding the relationship between leadership and the creation and sustainability of each school's inclusive culture. What emerged was a model of collaborative and collegial leadership comparable to that found at Betsy Miller. One individual held an official position of responsibility for the operation of each school. These *positional leaders* held the title of either Principal or Head Teacher.

Although each was instrumental in creating and supporting nonhierarchical organizational structures, none were laissez-faire. These positional leaders were not at all reluctant to be autocratic when faced with decisions that reflected values and beliefs central to inclusive education. For example, when discussing how teachers were selected for the school, the head of one British school explained, "People buy into the culture or don't stay. We indoctrinate." In describing his interactions with teachers during his first 2 years at the school, Joe Stephano explained how he consistently questioned teachers' referrals to special education and required all children to be included in general education classrooms.

> But initially, until it was established and institutionalized, I had to browbeat in particular some of the classroom teachers into accepting the fact that this was the way it was going to be done. And teachers are like all of us: They will wait and see if it's going to go away. So initially there was that notion, but I have sort of a pit bull mentality, so I would just keep saying it over and over again. Every Committee on Special Education meeting, whenever we talked about classifying a kid, I would sing the same tune. "What is classification going to give this kid that we can't give the kid already."

Each school employed the kinds of collaborative practices identified in the literature as central to inclusive schools and were organized in ways that required interaction and active participation among adults and children. Positional leaders did not micromanage their schools. Day to day responsibility for each school's operation was instead distributed among the staff. There was a clear understanding among the staff that in addition to the leadership provided by the head teacher or principal, some teachers had specific leadership roles and responsibilities. These *functional leaders* shared the inclusive philosophy and belief system of the positional leaders at their respective schools. At Betsy Miller, functional leadership was distributed among teachers and professional support staff who had been at the school for several years. They facilitated team meetings, worked in one another's classrooms, carried out staff development projects, and represented other staff at the schoolwide decision-making council, and mentored new teachers. At one British school, functional leadership was institutionalized by assigning teachers to specific roles as team leaders and curriculum coordinators, whose jobs included assisting other teachers with instruction and classroom management. At another inclusive school, functional leadership was more flexible and informal, with teachers assuming different leadership roles at different times.

The need to differentiate positional leaders from functional leaders reflects the expectation that one individual will respond to the demands of the hierarchical and bureaucratic educational systems in which their respective schools operate. Positional leaders are responsible for organizing and managing their schools and held accountable by centralized, external management systems for the performance of staff and students. Coupled with their commitment to inclusive education, these demands motivated the positional leaders of inclusive schools to initiate and develop nonhierarchical organizational systems and structures. They all understood that sustaining their respective schools' inclusive cultures required managing demands and requirements emanating from outside the school. Reconciling demands from within the school with sometimes contradictory external mandates required a good deal of political understanding and negotiation skills. The stress this created took its toll on each of these individuals. The shared and unique features of positional and functional leadership found at these inclusive schools are summarized in Figure 7.1.

A theme running through this analysis of leadership practice was that leadership is embedded in the culture of a school. In each setting, central to both sustaining inclusive educational practice in general and leadership in particular was an uncompromising commitment to principles of inclusion among both positional and functional leaders. The development of more inclusive approaches was not a mechanical process in which any one specific organizational restructuring or the introduction of a particular practice generated increased levels of student participation. Rather, the de-

FIGURE 7.1. A Comparative Analysis of Leadership in Inclusive Schools

I. Leadership features shared by "positional" and "functional" leaders

Uncompromising commitment to inclusive education
Collaborative interpersonal style
Problem solving and conflict resolution skills
Understanding and appreciation for the expertise of others
Supportive relationships with staff

II. Roles unique to "positional" leaders

Initiate and support nonhierarchical organizational systems and structures
  within the school
Responsibility for managing demands and requirements emanating from
  outside the school

III. Roles unique to "functional" leaders

Responsibility for collaborating with and supporting colleagues in instruction
  and classroom management

velopment of an inclusive culture required a shared commitment by the entire staff to processes that produced an overall enhancement of involvement by all participants.

Another aspect of school culture that emerged across these settings was the significance of collaboration. The willingness and ability of staff with different specializations to work together was seen as essential for blending support services and making them available to all children. Collaboration was both a form of practice and a manifestation of the inclusive values of these schools as they attempted to create a community in which all individuals—staff and students—were valued. Within this context, leadership became redefined and distributed, reinforcing a sense of community and of mutual trust within which it was embedded. These findings are similar to those of other researchers who report joint problem solving as a feature of their case studies of inclusive schools (Ainscow, 1999; Dyson & Millward, 2000). Hunt et al. (2000) also describe the collaborative development in which school staffs engaged. Responding to student diversity requires school staff to move beyond established practices; that in turn demands a process of learning about new practices and a willingness to struggle. These processes take place most effectively within a collaborative context.

The collaborative nature of inclusive school cultures has clear implications for leadership and decision making. First, it requires strong school leaders, whether teachers or principals. Second, these individuals must be committed to inclusive values and to promoting and supporting collaboration. In each of the schools I visited, positional leaders modeled collaborative practices in their everyday interactions with staff as well by developing formal and informal opportunities for staff to collaborate with one another. The importance of collaborative processes point to the importance of distributed leadership and participative decision making in managing inclusive schools.

Quakie's recollection of Joe's role in the transformation of Betsy Miller supports this analysis. In the following statement, she describes how he supported the development of functional leadership among teachers:

> By year three, it was really about transforming the school and not just a classroom here and there. It was a slow, methodical plan. First of all, it took my becoming an administrator to become aware of this: Joe was not afraid of being an administrator. A lot of administrators are. When he saw there were faculty members that weren't committed to all children in this building, they had to go. It was as simple as that. He would say, every year, "I'll get two more this year." He was able to coax them into environments that were more acceptable for them. And so he really did it so that we were always replacing them with staff that not only wanted to be here but also were committed to upping their cultural competency and their literacy and maybe didn't know where to go or how to do it, but wanted to learn.
>
> So we transformed the staff so that we had a group of people who were ripe to learn. He was quite skilled in bringing in not only the right outside people to facilitate that, but using the expertise of the staff in the building to take on leadership roles, where we could build a mission together as a faculty. So there was a time when we were truly all on the same page about where we were headed as a school, what our vision was for all kids in this building, and breaking down the walls around class and those other barriers. He was absolutely a genius at helping teachers discover within themselves their own power and ability to save a life. And that's how he saw it: "We are in the business of saving lives." Not just teaching basic skills. Anyone can do that. We're saving lives because if these kids don't make it here, these are the kids we are going to read about in the paper. He helped us see that. We never forgot that and that was always a part of our mission. We could always fall back on the mission as a group.

IMPLICATIONS FOR PROGRESSIVE REFORM
IN THE TWENTY-FIRST CENTURY

The current reform agenda in the United States is dominated by an obsession to create a uniform and standardized education system. By attaching educational funding to this agenda, the federal government is diminishing the power of public school systems to resist uniformity, thinly disguised in demands for accountability. School systems are responding to these pressures by putting even greater demands on teachers and principals, challenging their ability to create caring school and classroom communities, and requiring teachers to not question mandates calling for all children to learn the same things, at the same time, in the same way. Teachers are expected to neither question the values and beliefs underlying these requirements nor recognize the way those beliefs support a monocultural view of American society and undermine the sustainability of democratic educational institutions. In spite of pressure for conformity, many teachers, including those new to the profession, maintain a belief in the ideals expressed by teachers at Betsy Miller. Their continuing commitment to putting children at the center of the educational decisions can be heard in their stories. These narratives provide examples of resistance that give the lie to images of passive, obedient, and sexually repressed "schoolmarms" (Prentice & Theobald, 1991).

But why should teachers and administrators take the risk of challenging so deeply entrenched and impermeable a system? Why should teacher education programs prepare teachers to operate in ways that work against dominant educational paradigms? Isn't learning how to provide systematic group or individual instruction following a prescribed curriculum, textbook, or the Individual Education Plan for a child with special educational needs enough of a challenge? If children are provided instruction that is exclusively teacher directed and focused on skill development do well on high-stakes tests, why should principals encourage teachers to create inclusive classroom communities? Why should teachers promote student choice when that might lead to less certainty about test scores? The answer is simple: following the current educational agenda will fail to prepare students who take an active role in shaping their future as democratic citizens.

Historical investigations of women's roles in the development of public education document how women's commitments to social justice have shaped their decisions to become teachers and sustained a vision of progressive education during even more difficult times than those teachers face today. Holmes and Weiss (1995) describe the lives of nineteenth-century women who became teachers not only because it was one of the only acceptable professions they could enter, but also out of a commitment to progressive social values. For example, many women attending the first normal school that opened in 1839 in Lexington, Massachusetts, were influenced by transcendental philosophy, and supported women's suffrage and the abolition of slavery. For the school's founder, Cyrus Pierce, and women attending the school, universal public education was a vehicle for promoting social justice. Pedagogical practices were connected to progressive ideals and focused on "learning by doing, the value of reasoning over memorization, the importance of observation and child study, discipline without punishment, and learning tied to common experiences" (p. 37).

Electa Lincoln and Ellen Hyde, two women who attended the Model School, would be the first two principals after Pierce left. Both were committed to education as a vehicle for promoting social justice. In 1848 Electa Lincoln began integrating women's issues and abolition into the curriculum and advocated for the inclusion of African American women in the women's movement. Ellen Hyde continued to integrate both Pierce's pedagogical ideas and Lincoln's commitment to human rights and women's suffrage into the preparation of new teachers (1875–1898). She would expand the school's outreach to include Native and African Americans. Their school created a learning laboratory for teachers built on an instructional philosophy that would be articulated and practiced for more than 150 years, in spite of continued attacks from fundamentalist religious groups, conservative politicians, and business interests.

Throughout the twentieth century, sustaining progressive school reform has continued to require overcoming what seem like insurmountable obstacles. The stories of Betsy Miller's teachers, like those of their foresisters, demonstrate that teachers' commitments to social justice continue into the twenty-first century, in spite of political obstruction and an ever-increasing educational bureaucracy. The current focus on accountability has created even more demeaning and stressful working conditions than those faced by teachers who began shaping Betsy Miller's culture in 1987. Sustaining commitments to creating public education systems that place children and not political rhetoric at the center of education continues to be a difficult and unrewarded task for teachers. It will require feisty women and men, like those at Betsy Miller, who are willing to become heroic teacher-leaders, collaborating to create inclusive school cultures built on foundations of compassionate care.

References

Ainscow, M. (1999). *Understanding the development of inclusive schools.* London: Falmer.

Anderson, G. L. (1998). Towards authentic participation: Deconstructing the discourses of participatory reforms in education. *American Educational Research Journal, 35*(4), 571–603.

Antler, J., & Biklen, S. K. (Eds.). (1990). *Changing education: Women as radicals and conservators.* Albany: State University of New York Press.

Armstrong, T. (1993). *Multiple intelligences in the classroom.* Alexandria, VA: Association for Supervision and Curriculum Development.

Bailey, J., & du Plessis, D. (1997). Understanding principals' attitudes towards inclusive schooling. *Journal of Educational Administration, 35*(5), 428–438.

Barth, R. (1990). *Improving schools from within: Teachers, parents and principals can make a difference.* San Francisco: Jossey-Bass.

Bauer, A. M., & Lynch, E. M. (Eds.). (1993). *Children who challenge the system.* Norwood, NJ: Ablex.

Bauwens, J., & Hourcade, J. J. (1995). *Cooperative teaching: rebuilding the schoolhouse for all students.* Austin, TX: Pro-Ed.

Belenky, M., Clinchy, B., Goldberger, N. J., & Tarule, J. (1986). *Women's ways of knowing.* New York: Basic Books.

Berk, L. E., & Winsler, A. (1995). *Scaffolding children's learning: Vygotsky and early childhood education.* Washington, DC: National Association for the Education of Young Children.

Berres, M., Ferguson, D., Knoblock, P., & Wood, C. (Eds.). (1996). *Creating tomorrow's schools today: Stories of inclusion, change, and renewal.* New York: Teachers College Press.

Biklen, D. (1985). *Achieving the complete school: Strategies for effective mainstreaming.* New York: Teachers College Press.

Biklen, S. K. (1995). *School work: Gender and the cultural construction of teaching.* New York: Teachers College Press.

Bogdan, R., & Kugelmass, J. W. (1984). Case studies of mainstreaming: A symbolic interactionist approach to special schooling. In L. Barton & S. Tomlinson (Eds.), *Special education and social interests* (pp. 173–191). New York: Nichols.

Booth, T., & Ainscow, M. (Eds.). (1998). *From them to us: An international study of inclusion in education.* London: Routledge.

Borman, G. D., Hewes, G. M., Overman, L. T., & Brown, S. (2003). Comprehensive school reform and achievement: A meta-analysis. *Review of Educational Research, 73*(2), 125–230.

Burman, E. (1994). *Deconstructing developmental psychology.* New York: Routledge.

Campbell, J. (1949). *The hero with a thousand faces.* New York: MJF Books.

Campbell, L., Campbell, B., & Dickinson, D. (1996). *Teaching and learning through multiple intelligences.* Needham Heights, MA: Allyn & Bacon.

Carini, P. F. (2001). *Starting strong: A different look at children, schools, and standards.* New York: Teachers College Press.

Carlson, R. V. (1996). *Reframing and reform: Perspectives on organizations, leadership and school change.* White Plains, NY: Longman.

Casey, K. (1993). *I answer with my life: Life histories of women teachers working for social change.* New York: Routledge.

Clifford, J. (1986). Introduction: Partial truths. In J. Clifford & G. E. Marcus (Eds.), *Writing culture: The poetics and politics of ethnography* (pp. 1–26). Berkeley: University of California Press.

Coffey, A., & Delamont, S. (2000). *Feminism and the classroom teacher.* London: Falmer Press.

Connelly, F. M., & Clandinin, D. J. (1988). *Teachers as curriculum planners: Narratives of experience.* New York: Teachers College Press.

Dalai Lama, & Cutler, H. C. (2000). *The art of happiness: A handbook for living.* New York: Penguin Putnam.

Deal, T. E., & Peterson, K. D. (1999). *Shaping school culture: The heart of leadership.* San Francisco: Jossey-Bass.

Delpit, L. D. (1986). Skills and other dilemmas of a progressive black educator. *Harvard Educational Review, 56*(4), 379–385.

Delpit, L. D. (1988). The silenced dialogue: Power and pedagogy in educating other people's children. *Harvard Educational Review, 58*(3), 280–298.

Dettmer, P. A., Dyck, N. T., & Thurston, L. P. (1996). *Consultation, collaboration, and teamwork for students with special needs.* Newton, MA: Allyn & Bacon.

Dewey, J. (1938). *Experience and education.* New York: Macmillan

Docking, J. (Ed.). (2000). *New Labour's policies for schools: Raising the standard?* London: David Fulton.

Dorsch, N. G. (1998). *Community, collaboration and collegiality in school reform: An odyssey toward connections.* Albany: State University of New York Press.

Dyson, A., & Millward, A. (Eds.). (2000). *Schools and special needs: Issues of innovation and inclusion.* London: Paul Chapman.

Education for All Handicapped Children Act of 1975, Pub. L. No. 94-142 (August 23, 1975).

Elementary and Secondary Education Act of 1965, Title I regulation amendments. *Federal Register* (60 FR 34800) (July 3, 1995).

Evans, J. (1995). *Feminist theory today: An introduction to second-wave feminism.* Thousand Oaks, CA: Sage.

Evans, R. (1996). *The human side of school change: Reform, resistance and the real-life problems of innovation.* San Francisco: Jossey-Bass.

Fielding, M. (1999). Radical collegiality: Affirming teaching as an inclusive professional practice. *Australian Educational Researcher, 26*(2), 1–34.

Flinders, D. J., & Bowers, C. A. (1990). *Responsive teaching: An ecological approach to classroom patterns of language, culture, and thought.* New York: Teachers College Press.

Foxfire Fund. (1991). The Foxfire approach: Perspectives and core practices. *Hands-On: A Journal for Teachers, 41,* 3–4.

Franklin, B. M. (1994). *From "backwardness" to "at-risk": Childhood learning difficulties and the contradictions of school reform.* Albany: State University of New York Press.

Freedman, S. (1990). Weeding women out of "women's true profession." In J. Antler & S. K. Biklen (Eds.), *Changing education: Women as radicals and conservators* (pp. 239–256). Albany: State University of New York Press.

Friend, M., & Cook, L. (1996). *Interactions: Collaboration skills for professionals* (2nd. ed.). White Plains, NY : Longman.

Fullan, M. (1991). *The new meaning of educational change* (2nd. ed.). New York: Teachers College Press.

Fullan, M. (2001). *Leading in a culture of change.* San Francisco: Jossey-Bass.

Fullan, M., & Hargreaves, A. (1996). *What's worth fighting for in your school?* New York: Teachers College Press.

Fuller, B., & Clark, P. (1994). Raising school effects while ignoring culture? Local conditions and the influence of classroom tools, rules and pedagogy. *Review of Educational Research, 64*(1), 119–157.

Geertz, C. (1973). *The interpretation of cultures.* New York: Basic Books.

Gilligan, C. (1982). *In a different voice: Psychological theory and women's development.* Cambridge, MA: Harvard University Press.

Greene, M. (1995). *Releasing the imagination: Essays on education, the arts, and social change.* San Francisco: Jossey-Bass.

Grumet, M. (1988). *Bitter milk: Women and teaching.* Amherst: University of Massachusetts Press.

Guzman, N. (1997). Leadership for successful inclusive schools: A study of principal behaviors. *Journal of Educational Administration, 35*(5), 439–450.

Halford, S., & Leonard, P. (2001). *Gender, power and organizations.* Hampshire, UK: Palgrave.

Hall, E. T. (1983). *The dance of life: The other dimension of time.* New York: Doubleday.

Hargreaves, A. (1982). *Two cultures of schooling: The case of middle schools.* London: Falmer Press.

Hargreaves, A. (1994). *Changing teachers, changing times: Teachers' work and culture in the postmodern age.* New York: Teachers College Press.

Henry, M. (1996). *Parent-school collaboration: Feminist organizational structures and school leadership.* Albany: State University of New York Press.

Herbert, K. S., & Hatch, T. (2001, April). *Keeping up the good work: Developing and sustaining capacity for school improvement.* Paper presented at the meeting of the American Educational Research Association, Seattle, Washington.

Himley, M., & Carini, P. F. (Eds.). (2000). *From another angle: Children's strengths and school standards.* New York: Teachers College Press.

Holmes, M., & Weiss, B. J. (1995). *Lives of women public school teachers.* New York: Garland.

Hord, S. M., Rutherford, W. L., Huling-Austin, L., & Hall, G. E. (1987). *Taking charge of change.* Alexandria, VA: Association for Supervision and Curriculum Development.

Hunt, P., Hirose-Hatae, A., Doering, K., & Goetz, L. (2000). "Community" is what I think everyone is talking about. *Remedial and Special Education, 21*(5), 305–317.

Individuals with Disabilities Education Act of 1990, Pub. L. No. 101-476 (October 30, 1990).

Ingram, P. D. (1997). Leadership behaviors of principals in inclusive educational settings. *Journal of Educational Administration, 35*(5), 411–427.

Johnson, I. (2002). "My eyes have been open": White teachers and racial awareness. *Journal of Teacher Education, 53*(2), 153–167.

Jung, C. G. (1958). Aion. In V. S. Laszlo (Ed.), *Psyche and symbol: A selection from the writings of C. G. Jung* (pp. 1–60). Garden City, NY: Doubleday Anchor. (Original work published 1951)

Katz, M. (1971). *Class, bureaucracy and change: The illusion of educational change in America.* New York: Praeger.

Keogh, B. K. (1988). Improving services for problem learners: Rethinking and restructuring. *Journal of Learning Disabilities, 21*(1), 19–22.

Kirp, D. L. (1992). Student classification, public policy, and the courts. In T. Hehir & T. Latus (Eds.), *Special education at the century's end: Evolution of theory and practice since 1970* (pp. 3–45). Reprint Series no. 23. Cambridge, MA: Harvard Educational Review. (Original work published 1973)

Knoblock, P. (Ed.). (1982). *Teaching and mainstreaming autistic children.* Denver, CO: Love.

Knoblock, P. (1996). Environments for everyone: Community building and restructuring. In M. Berres, D. Ferguson, P. Knoblock, & C. Wood (Eds.), *Creating tomorrow's schools today: Stories of inclusion, change, and renewal* (pp. 167–187). New York: Teachers College Press.

Kreisberg, S. (1992). *Transforming power: Domination, empowerment and education.* Albany: State University of New York Press.

Kugelmass, J. W. (1987). *Behavior, bias, and handicaps: Labeling the emotionally disturbed child.* New Brunswick, NJ: Transaction Books.

Kugelmass, J. W. (2000). Subjective experience and the preparation of activist teachers: Confronting the mean old snapping turtle and the great big bear. *Teaching and Teacher Education, 16*(3), 179–194.

Kugelmass, J. W. (2001). Collaboration and compromise in creating and sustaining an inclusive school. *International Journal of Inclusive Education, 5*(1), 47–65.

Kugelmass, J. W., & Ainscow, M. (2003, April). *Leadership for inclusive education: a comparison of international practices.* Paper presented at the meeting of the American Educational Research Association, Chicago.

Kugelmass, J. W., & Rainforth, B. (2003). Searching for a pedagogy of success. In B. Rainforth & J. W. Kugelmass (Eds.), *Curriculum and instruction for all learners: Blending systematic and constructivist approaches in inclusive elementary schools* (pp. 3–25). Baltimore, MD: Paul H. Brookes.

Kunc, N. (2000). Rediscovering the right to belong. In R. A. Villa & J. S. Thousand (Eds.), *Restructuring for caring and effective education: Piecing the puzzle together* (2nd ed., pp. 77–92). Baltimore: Paul H. Brookes.

Ladson-Billings, G. (1994). *The dreamkeepers: Successful teachers of African American children.* San Francisco: Jossey-Bass.

Lambert, L., Walker, D., Zimmerman, D. P., Cooper, J. E., Lambert, M. D., Gardner, M. E., & Szabo, M. (2002). *The constructivist leader* (2nd ed.). New York: Teachers College Press.

Larry P. v. Riles, 343 F. Supp. 1306 (N.D. Cal. 1972).

Laszlo, V. S. (Ed.). (1958). *Psyche and symbol: A selection from the writings of C. G. Jung.* Garden City, NY: Doubleday Anchor.

Lave, J., & Wenger, E. (1991). *Situated learning: Legitimate peripheral participation.* Cambridge, UK: Cambridge University Press.

Leithwood, K., Jantzi, D., & Steinbach, R. (1999). *Changing leadership for changing times.* Buckingham, UK: Open University Press.

Lieberman, A. (Ed.). (1995). *The work of restructuring schools: Building from the ground up.* New York: Teachers College Press.

Lincoln, Y., & Guba, E. (1985). *Naturalistic inquiry.* Newbury Park, CA: Sage.

Little, J. W. (1982). Norms of collegiality and experimentation: Working conditions of school success. *American Education Research Journal, 19*(3), 325–340.

Little, J. W. (1990). The persistence of privacy: Autonomy and initiative in teachers' professional relations. *Teachers College Record, 91*(4), 509–536.

Lipsky, D. A., & Gartner, A. (1996). *School reform and inclusive education.* Baltimore: Paul H. Brookes.

Luke, C., & Gore, J. (1992). *Feminisms and critical pedagogy.* New York: Routledge.

Lytle, J. H. (1992). Is special education serving minority students: A response to Singer and Butler. In T. Hehir & T. Latus (Eds.), *Special education at the century's end: Evolution of theory and practice since 1970* (pp. 191–197). Reprint Series no. 23. Cambridge, MA: Harvard Educational Review. (Original work published 1988)

Macmillan, D. L., Keogh, B. K., & Jones, R. L. (1986). Special education research on mildly handicapped learners. In M. C. Wittrock (Ed.), *Handbook of research on teaching* (3rd ed., pp. 686–724). New York: Macmillan.

Maehr, M. L., & Midgley, C. (1996). *Transforming school culture.* Boulder, CO.: Westview Press.

Maeroff, G, I. (1988). *The empowerment of teachers: Overcoming the crisis of confidence.* New York: Teachers College Press.

Mallory, B., & New, R. (1996). *Diversity and developmentally appropriate practice.* New York: Teachers College Press.

Manset, G., & Semmel, M. I. (1997). Are inclusive programs for students with mild disabilities effective? A comparative review of model programs. *The Journal of Special Education, 31*(20), 155–180.

Marcus, G., & Fischer, M. J. (1986). *Anthropology as cultural critique: An experiment in the human sciences.* Chicago: University of Chicago Press.

Meyen, E. L., & Skrtic, T. M. (1995). *Special education and student disability: Traditional, emerging and alternative perspectives.* Denver: Love.

Miller, J. L. (1990). *Creating spaces and finding voices: Teachers collaborating for empowerment.* Albany: State University of New York Press.

Muncey, D. E., & McQuillan, P. J. (1996). *Reform and resistance in schools and classrooms.* New Haven, CT: Yale University Press.

Munro, P. (1998). *Subject to fiction: Women teachers' life history narratives and the cultural politics of resistance.* Buckingham, UK: Open University Press.

New York State Education Department. VESID. (1999). *Pocketbook of goals and results for individuals with disabilities.* Retrieved April 19, 2004, from http://www.vesid.nysed.gov/pocketbook/home/html

No Child Left Behind Act of 2002, Pub. L. No. 107-110. *Federal Register* (67 FR 50986) (Aug. 6, 2002).

Noddings, N. (1984). *Caring: A feminine approach to ethics and moral education.* Berkeley: University of California Press.

Polanyi, M. (1966). *The tacit dimension.* New York: Doubleday.

Poplin, M. S. (1988). The reductionistic fallacy in learning disabilities: Replicating the past by reducing the present. *Journal of Learning Disabilities, 21*(7), 401–416.

Poplin, M. S., & Cousin, P. T. (Eds.). (1996). *Alternative views of learning disabilities: Issues for the twenty-first century.* Austin, TX: Pro-Ed.

Pounder, D. G. (1998). *Restructuring schools for collaboration: Promises and pitfalls.* Albany: State University of New York Press.

Prentice, A., & Theobald, M. R. (1991). *Women who taught: Perspectives on the history of women and teaching.* Toronto: University of Toronto Press.

Pugach, M., & Johnson, L. (1995). *Collaborative practitioners, collaborative schools.* Denver, CO: Love.

Rainforth, B., & Kugelmass, J. W. (Eds.). (2003). *Curriculum and instruction for all learners: Blending systematic and constructivist approaches in inclusive elementary schools.* Baltimore, MD: Paul Brookes.

Rainforth, B., & York-Barr, J. (Eds.). (1997). *Collaborative teams for students with severe disabilities: Integrating therapy and educational services.* Baltimore: Paul H. Brookes.

Regenspan, B. (2002). *Parallel practices: Social justice–focused teacher education and the elementary school classroom.* New York: Peter Lang.

Rhodes, L., & Dudley-Marling, C. (1988). *Readers and writers with a difference: A holistic approach to teaching learning-disabled and remedial students.* Portsmouth, NH: Heinemann.

Riehl, C. J. (2000). The principal's role in creating inclusive schools for diverse students: a review of normative, empirical, and critical literature on the practice of educational administration. *Review of Educational Research, 70*(1), 55–81.

Ruddick, S. (1999). Maternal thinking. In M. Pearsall (Ed.), *Women and values: Readings in recent feminist philosophy* (pp. 368–378). Belmont, CA: Wadsworth. (Original work published 1980)

Sarason, S. B. (1996). *Revisiting "The culture of school and the problem of change."* New York: Teachers College Press.

Sergiovanni, T. J. (1992). *Moral leadership: Getting to the heart of school improvement.* San Francisco: Jossey-Bass.

Sergiovanni, T. J. (1994). *Building community in schools.* San Francisco: Jossey-Bass.

Shakeshaft, C. (1998). Wild patience and bad fit: Assessing the impact of affirmative action on women in school administration. *Educational Researcher, 27*(9), 10–12.

Shea, T. M., & Bauer, A. M. (1995). *An introduction to special education: A social systems perspective.* Madison, WI: Brown & Benchmark.

Skrtic, T. (1991a). *Behind special education: A critical analysis of professional culture and school organization.* Denver, CO: Love.

Skrtic, T. (1991b). The special education paradox: Equity as the way to excellence. *Harvard Educational Review, 61*(2), 148–206.

Sleeter, C. E., & Grant, C. A. (1999). *Making choices for multicultural education: Five approaches to race, class, and gender.* New York: John Wiley & Sons.

Smith, S. C., & Scott, J. J. (1990). *The collaborative school: A work environment for effective instruction.* Eugene, OR: ERIC Clearinghouse on Educational Management.

A special-ed warning for New York [Editorial]. (1998, December 2). *New York Times,* p. 26A.

Spillane, J. P., Halverson, R., & Diamond, J. B. (2001). Investigating school leadership practice. *Educational Researcher, 30*(3), 23–28.

Spooner, F., & Johnson, L. (Eds.). (1996). *Teacher Education and Special Education* [Special issue]. *19*(3).

Stainback, S., & Stainback, W. (Eds.). (1991). *Curriculum considerations in inclusive classrooms: Facilitating learning for all students.* Baltimore: Paul H. Brookes.

Stainback, S., & Stainback, W. (Eds.). (1996). *Inclusion: A guide for educators.* Baltimore: Paul H. Brookes.

Straub, G. (2000). *The rhythm of compassion: Caring for self, connecting with society.* Boston: Tuttle Publishing.

Swadener, B. B., & Lubeck, S. (Eds.). (1995). *Children and families "at promise": Deconstructing the discourse of risk.* Albany: State University of New York Press.

Trent, S. C., Artiles, A. J., & Englert, C. S. (1998). From deficit thinking to social constructivism: A review of theory, research, and practice in special education. *Review of Research in Education, 23,* 277–307.

Tyack, D., & Cuban, L. (1995). *Tinkering toward utopia: A century of public school reform.* Cambridge, MA: Harvard University Press.

Udvari-Solnar, A., & Keyes, M. W. (2000). Leadership toward inclusive reform: "We're on the train and left the station, but haven't gotten to the next stop." In R. A. Villa & J. S. Thousand (Eds.), *Restructuring for caring and effective education: Putting the puzzle together* (pp. 428–452). Baltimore, MD: Paul Brookes.

UNESCO. (1997). *Inclusive schools and community support programs.* Report 1996, First Phase 1997. Paris, France: UNESCO.

UNESCO. (2000). *Inclusive education and education for all: A challenge and a vision.* Section for special needs education. Paris, France: UNESCO.

U. S. Bureau of the Census. (2000). United States Census, 2000. http://www.census .gov/main/cen2000.html

Vitello, S. J., & Mithaug, D. E. (Eds.). (1998). *Inclusive schooling: National and international perspectives.* Mahwah, NJ: Lawrence Erlbaum.

Vygotsky, L. S. (1978). *Mind and society.* Cambridge, MA: Harvard University Press.

Walkerdine, V. (1984). Developmental psychology and the child-centered pedagogy: the insertion of Piaget into early education. In J. Henriques, W. Hollway, C. Urwin, C. Venn, & V. Walkerdine (Eds.), *Changing the subject: Psychology, social regulation and subjectivity* (pp. 153–202). London: Methuen.

Weiler, K. (1988). *Women teaching for change: Gender, class and power.* New York: Bergin & Garvey.

Wenger, E. (1998). *Communities of practice: Learning, meaning, and identity.* Cambridge, UK: Cambridge University Press.

Wideen, M., Mayer-Smith, J., & Moon, B. (1998). A critical analysis on the research on learning to teach: Making the case for an ecological perspective on inquiry. *Review of Educational Research, 68*(2), 130–178.

Wiggins, G. (1989). A true test: Toward more authentic and equitable assessment. *Phi Delta Kappan, 70,* 703–713.

Wiggins, G. (1991). Standards not standardization: Evoking quality student work. *Educational Leadership, 48*(5), 18–25.

Witherell, C., & Noddings, N. (Eds.). (1991). *Stories lives tell: Narrative and dialogue in education.* New York: Teachers College Press.

Wolf, M. (1992). *A thrice-told tale: Feminism, postmodernism, and ethnographic responsibility.* Stanford, CA: Stanford University Press.

Worthen, B. R. (1993). Critical issues that will determine the future of alternative assessment. *Phi Delta Kappan, 74*(6), 444–454.

Index

About the Author

Judy W. Kugelmass is Associate Professor in the Division of Education, School of Education and Human Development, Binghamton University (SUNY), where she teaches and coordinates the masters degree program in teacher preparation for inclusive childhood education, supervises doctoral student research, and offers courses in qualitative research and educational ethnography. She has taught at Cornell University, Hobart and William Smith Colleges, and Goddard College. Her understanding of the significance of sociocultural contexts in the development of inclusive schools reflects extensive experience with schools in the United States and abroad. She has worked with teachers, administrators, and higher education faculty in Indonesia, Portugal, the United Kingdom, Lithuania, Ukraine, and several other Eastern European countries. Her research in the development of inclusive schools explores issues related to leadership, teacher preparation, collaboration with families, school culture, and the development of effective pedagogical practices. Her book (co-edited with Beverly Rainforth), *Curriculum and Instruction for ALL Learners: Blending Systematic and Constructivist Practices in Inclusive Elementary Schools* (Paul Brookes), examines debates surrounding instructional approaches for schools and classrooms serving diverse student populations and provides in-depth examples of effective practices.

Dr. Kugelmass served as coordinator of the Foxfire Teacher Outreach Network in New York State (1990–1994), in addition to being a teacher of young children, a school psychologist, and an administrator of early intervention programs. She lives with her husband in the midst of the Finger Lakes National Forest in upstate New York State. Her proudest achievements are her son, daughter, and two grandchildren.